MW01034272

PHILIPPIANS

PHILIPPIANS: FINDING JOY WHEN LIFE IS HARD

Josiah D. Bancroft IV

STUDY GUIDE WITH LEADER'S NOTES

New
Growth
Press
newgrowthpress.com

New Growth Press, Greensboro, NC 27401
newgrowthpress.com
Copyright © 2023 by Josiah D. Bancroft IV

All rights reserved. No part of this publication may be reproduced, stored in a retrieval system, or transmitted in any form by any means, electronic, mechanical, photocopy, recording, or otherwise, without the prior permission of the publisher, except as provided by USA copyright law.

Scripture quotations are from The ESV® Bible (The Holy Bible, English Standard Version®), copyright © 2001 by Crossway, a publishing ministry of Good News Publishers. Used by permission. All rights reserved.

Cover Design: Dan Stelzer
Interior Typesetting and eBook: Lisa Parnell
Exercises and Application Questions: Jack Klumpenhower

ISBN: 978-1-64507-351-2 (Print)
ISBN: 978-1-64507-352-9 (E-book)

Printed in the United States of America

30 29 28 27 26 25 24 23   1 2 3 4 5

For Barbara,

who walks with me as we learn
to rejoice in Jesus every step of the way.

✳ ✳ ✳ ✳

A special thanks to Anna Madsen and Patric Knaak,
who helped me along with this project in remarkable ways.

CONTENTS

INTRODUCTION

The epistle to the Philippians is known for its expressions of joy. Given the context from which Paul is writing—a Roman jail—hearing him speak about joy is nothing short of remarkable. Despite his dire circumstances, what was his exhortation to the Philippians? Rejoice! All through the letter Paul explains how, because of what Christ has done, they too can experience his joy. He repeats himself so often that joy is clearly one of the themes of the letter.

But joy is not the center of Paul's message. The center is Jesus Christ. The further into the letter we get, the more we will see that Philippians is all about Jesus. Paul will remind the Philippian church *who Christ is* and *who they are in Christ*. He will teach them how to *believe in Christ* and *walk with Christ*. He will point to the supernatural joy that does not depend on circumstances but comes from the *Spirit of Christ* as we press on in the life of faith.

By studying Philippians, you are stepping into that same experience. Paul's desire is that his readers live as citizens of the heavenly realm, where Jesus is King, and where their increasing confidence *in him* compels them all the more to proclaim and live out the gospel without fear. So as you read this letter, receive it and respond to it with gospel faith. Gospel faith makes you part of the story, centered on Jesus, believing that the things Paul described in the first century are also yours today. Paul is not just writing to the Philippian church he started; he is also writing to you, wherever you are today. As you read and study, the Holy Spirit will help you understand and will encourage you to believe it is true and valuable—not just generally, but *for you specifically*. He will remind you that God's promises are for you and enable your relationship with God to flow from the gospel.

HOW TO USE THIS STUDY

This study guide will help you experience Philippians within a group. Paul wrote his letter not to a single believer, but to an entire church family. It is meant to be studied alongside other believers. Doing this lets you benefit from what God is also teaching them, and it gives you their encouragement as you apply what you learn.

Each participant should have one of these study guides to join in reading and be able to work through the exercises during that part of the study. The study leader should read through both the lesson and the leader's notes in the back of this book before each lesson begins. No other preparation or homework is required.

There are nine lessons in this study guide. Each lesson will take about an hour to complete, perhaps a bit more if your group is large, and will include these elements:

BIG IDEA. This is a summary of the main point of the lesson.

BIBLE CONVERSATION. Your group will read a passage from Philippians and discuss it. As the heading suggests, the Bible conversation questions are intended to spark a conversation rather than generate correct answers. In most cases, the questions will have several possible good answers. The leader's notes at the back of this book provide some insights, but don't just turn there for the "right answer." At times, you may want to see what the notes say, but always try to answer for yourselves first by thinking about the Bible passage.

ARTICLE. This is the main teaching section of the lesson, written by this book's author.

DISCUSSION. The discussion questions following the article will help you apply the teaching to your life. Again, there will be several good ways to answer each question.

EXERCISE. The exercise is a section you will complete on your own during group time. You can write in the book if that helps you. You will then share some of what you learned with the group. If the group is large, it may help to split up to share the results of the exercise and to pray, so that everyone has a better opportunity to participate.

WRAP-UP AND PRAYER. Prayer is a critical part of the lesson because, as you will be studying, "It is God who works in you, both to will and to work for his good pleasure" (Philippians 2:13). Your spiritual growth through this study will come by God's power and kindness, not by your self-effort. Your group will be asking God to do that good work.

By studying Philippians, you are about to encounter both Paul's gospel proclamation and his transformative experience. Writing to friends from prison, only a few years from his martyrdom, Paul boasts in Christ Jesus and boldly declares, "Rejoice in the Lord!" Whatever wonders and worries God has brought into your life today, expect to be able to say the same.

1

IDENTITY

BIG IDEA

Our identity is defined primarily by our relationship with Jesus Christ, and not by our actions, achievements, or struggles.

BIBLE CONVERSATION *20 MINUTES*

Philippians is a letter from the apostle Paul to the church he founded in the Roman colony of Philippi. Paul had formerly been a religious high-achiever. He had studied under celebrated Jewish teachers, practiced strict obedience, and persecuted the early Christians until he became a believer himself and was sent out as a missionary. On his second missionary trip, he was accompanied by Silas, Luke, and his young apprentice Timothy. The team crossed into Europe and came to Philippi in the northern part of modern-day Greece. The city was largely populated by retired Roman soldiers and was known for its patriotic nationalism.

The team soon met Lydia, a merchant and foreigner who worshipped God but had not heard the gospel of Jesus. Luke reports, "The Lord opened her heart to pay attention to what was said by Paul. And after she was baptized, and her household as well, she urged us, saying, 'If you have judged me to be faithful to the Lord, come to my house and stay." And she prevailed upon us" (Acts 16:14–15). But after Paul cast a demon out of a slave girl, he and Silas were attacked, beaten, and thrown into prison. As they were praying and singing to God at midnight, an earthquake shook the prison, loosening their chains and opening the doors. The jailer, anticipating the punishment he would receive for escaped prisoners, drew his sword to kill himself. But Paul called out and stopped him, assuring him no one had run.

> And the jailer called for lights and rushed in, and trembling with fear he fell down before Paul and Silas. Then he brought them out and said, "Sirs, what must I do to be saved?" And they said, "Believe in the Lord Jesus, and you will be saved, you and your household." And they spoke the word of the Lord to him and to all who were in his house. And he took them the same hour of the night and washed their wounds; and he was baptized at once, he and all his family. Then he brought them up into his house and set food before them. And he rejoiced along with his entire household that he had believed in God. (Acts 16:29–34)

The letter to the Philippians came years after that extraordinary start to the church, while Paul was in prison again, this time in Rome. Prisoners in that culture were not necessarily even fed by their guards, so the Philippian church had sent Paul a gift to help see to his needs. Paul responded with this letter to thank them for their friendship and support. With this context in mind, begin your study of Philippians by having someone read **Philippians 1:1–2** aloud. Then discuss the questions below:

Think about the merchant Lydia and the Roman jailer, and the loyalties they likely felt before becoming believers. What about their behavior after they believed stands out to you, and why?

In Philippians, notice the words Paul uses to describe himself, Timothy, and the everyday people in the church at Philippi. How would you feel if you were regularly called by those labels? Explain.

Look closely at the greeting in verse 2. What would you appreciate about being greeted that way, and why?

＊＊＊＊

Now read the following article, written by this book's author. Take turns reading aloud, switching readers at each paragraph break. When you finish, discuss the questions at the end of the article.

GOD'S HOLY PEOPLE

5 MINUTES

The beginning of Paul's letter to the Philippian church oozes warmth and affection. As someone who has served as a missionary for several decades and has been supported by multiple churches, I am privileged to have written my share of thank-you notes. I can tell you that this letter is no mere thank-you note written out of duty to a supporting congregation.

No, Paul's personal connection with the Philippians is obvious, and it makes sense given the church's incredible beginnings. The Philippians became not only Paul's supporters but also his friends for the rest of his life. This is because the gospel doesn't just bring us into eternal union with Christ, it also unites us with other believers in Jesus. "We are members one of another" (Ephesians 4:25).

Paul begins his letter like any writer of the day would: identifying himself, those with him, and those to whom he is writing. But he quickly brings in the foundation of his relationship with them—the gospel. Because God graciously rescued Paul from slavery to sin, he and his apprentice Timothy are now fundamentally and primarily servants (or slaves) of Christ Jesus.

For Paul, there is nothing that is not in, of, by, and for Christ Jesus. So, as he addresses this letter to his Philippian friends, he invokes their identity in Christ Jesus as well. The recipients of his letter are no longer primarily retired Roman soldiers, Jews, or formerly demon-possessed slave girls. Instead, Paul addresses them as *saints*. That word means they are God's holy people in Christ Jesus! This is their true and primary identity. It is what has bound them together.

When I was a boy, I was called Joe or "Little Joe" because I had my father's name. And I wanted to be a doctor just like him. But after I came to Christ and was in college, I remember very clearly asking to be called by my given name, Josiah. The name means "healed by God," and his love and grace now defined me in a new way. I still honored my father. He was a hero to me. But being called by my whole name, Josiah, pointed to my new eternal identity in Christ, healed by faith in the gospel. Even now, decades later, my name reminds me of who I am eternally, in light of the person and work of Jesus Christ.

This is what the gospel means for us too. Gospel faith brings a new identity. Now, through faith, our lives are wrapped up in the life of Jesus. As we trust in the coming, living, dying, and rising of Jesus for us, we are no longer just who the world says we are. We are not defined by who our family says we are. We are not primarily identified by our politics, our career, or our education. We are not even who *we* say we are! All these things are important, but they do not ultimately define us.

We are who *God* says we are. In another of Paul's letters, he says, "I have been crucified with Christ. . . . And the life I now live in the flesh I live by faith in the Son of God, who loved me and gave himself for me" (Galatians 2:20). For us, too, our primary identity is in our relationship with God through faith in Christ. This identity is revealed to us by God in Scripture. When we believe the gospel, we are who God says we are in Christ.

Because of Paul's insistence on the gospel, we can be sure that his "grace and peace" greeting to the Philippians is no ordinary salutation or religious convention. Here too, his goal is to root his readers constantly in the gospel. First, we have *grace*: our gospel identity comes to us wholly from God by his unmerited favor. This favor has reconciled us to him through the work of Christ. Further, we have *peace*: our new identity now wondrously gives us, who used to be God's enemies, peace with God.

Grace comes first because salvation is entirely of God, and peace that transcends all understanding is the result. The prophet Isaiah pointed to Christ as the Prince of Peace, because it was his punishment that secured peace for us. "Upon him was the chastisement that brought us peace, and with his wounds we are healed" (Isaiah 53:5). The promise of God's peace through the work of Christ is repeated throughout the New Testament as well, often accompanied by the promise of the very presence of Christ with us through faith.*

For us as believers, hearing "grace and peace" should be shorthand for the gospel. Paul's greeting to his beloved Philippians is a reminder that all of us have been plucked out of our wayward tendencies—our attempts to find life and peace through idols or self-generated righteousness. Like Paul and those who came to faith in Philippi, we have been put down on a new path. This path says that no matter where we go, or what we do, Christ Jesus is our life. His priorities are now ours, and his blessings are now ours as well. That is truly grace and peace.

DISCUSSION *10 MINUTES*

How mindful do you remain of the fact that Jesus is your life, whatever you are doing? Are there parts of your life where you feel more aware or less aware of this? Explain.

What especially warm relationships have you had that have been based first of all on a shared identity in Christ? Explain.

---

*See Luke 2:14; John 14:27; 16:33; 20:19.

Lesson

EXERCISE

WHO ARE YOU?

20 MINUTES

No matter how well you know that your core identity is in Christ, there likely will be times you tend to see yourself in some other way first. For this exercise, work on your own to think about how you answer the question "Who am I?" and what the Bible tells you about it. Complete both steps of the exercise below. Then, when the group is ready, discuss the questions at the end of the exercise together.

STEP 1: HOW YOU SEE YOUR IDENTITY. Let's use the people mentioned at the start of Paul's letter, plus some who were there when the Philippian church began, to think about identity. Note for yourself which of the following types of identity might sometimes feel defining to you.

☐ **The merchant.** I find my identity in my work or career, or in the reputation that comes with workplace or school success.

☐ **The Roman soldier.** I find my identity in my heritage, my national or political affiliation, or a cause I dutifully support.

☐ **The household member.** I find my identity in the family or community I belong to, or in its status, appearance, or way of doing things.

☐ **The slave girl.** I find my identity in a certain hurt I have suffered or lifestyle I have lived, or in some struggle or condition that seems to define my life.

☐ **The overseer or deacon.** I find my identity in a role I have within the church or some Christian ministry.

☐ **The religious achiever.** I find my identity in being spiritually devout, morally upstanding, or doctrinally right.

☐ **The young apprentice.** I find my identity in my youth or my age, or in my generation's way of earning approval or likability.

☐ **Other:** _____.

STEP 2: YOUR GREATER IDENTITY IN CHRIST. As with everyone connected to the Philippian church, your greater identity is in how you are joined to Jesus and his people. If you are a believer, you are a saint and a servant receiving grace and peace in Christ. This should define how you go about everything else. So now, read through the following list of truths about who you are in Christ that come from the rest of Paul's letter, and do the following:

1. Pick a few that most clearly show you how Jesus is a better identity than your lesser, other identities.

2. Pick <u>one</u> and read the passage from Philippians that goes with it. Be ready to share what you learned from that passage.

☐ **God in me.** God is at work in me to make me someone who loves others and brings glory to him (read Philippians 1:6–11).

☐ **Shame lifted.** I can serve Christ with honor, knowing that whatever happens, I belong to my King both in life and in death (read Philippians 1:20–23).

☐ **Engaged in the fight.** I am employed in *the* great struggle against sin and evil, on the side of Christ the winner (read Philippians 1:27–30).

☐ **Humility.** I am equipped to be the rarest kind of person, one who actually cares for others ahead of myself (read Philippians 2:3–5).

☐ **Shining light.** In the midst of a troubled world, I have a compelling mission and purpose worth living for or even dying for (read Philippians 2:15, 25–29).

☐ **Righteous record.** I rest in a perfectly righteous standing bestowed on me by God instead of an earned record that's a constant burden to maintain (read Philippians 3:8–9).

☐ **Citizenship in heaven.** I will be resurrected from the dead, rescued from shame and destruction, by my Savior who is coming to bring me into glory (read Philippians 3:18–20).

☐ **Joy.** I can be a person of deep thankfulness, peace, and contentment even in this life's hardest situations (read Philippians 4:4–7).

When the group is ready, share and explain your responses. What other identities sometimes feel bigger to you than who you are in Christ? How does the passage you read show you that Christ is your bigger and better identity?

WRAP-UP AND PRAYER *10 MINUTES*

As part of your group's first prayer time together, include prayers that your study of Philippians would be profitable, bringing you closer to Jesus and each other.

2

CONFIDENCE

BIG IDEA

As we anchor our identity in Christ, we can have hope that God will complete the good work he has begun in us.

BIBLE CONVERSATION *20 MINUTES*

The opening verses of Philippians gave us a sense of Paul's laser focus on the gospel, which gives believers a whole new identity anchored in Jesus. Now as Paul reflects on that reality, we will see his heartfelt joy bubble up in his prayer life—both prayers of thanks and prayers for God's work in the Philippians. This is in contrast to some bleak circumstances, as Paul is writing from prison in Rome.

Have someone read **Philippians 1:3–11** aloud. Then discuss the following questions:

What are some ways Paul is more inclusive or far-reaching in his desires and prayers than you might be? Explain.

Look at how Paul writes about his affection for the Philippians. If you want to have the same kind of affection for other believers, which of Paul's attitudes and underlying beliefs will you have to adopt?

What do you like most about the specific requests in Paul's prayer in verses 9–11? Explain why.

****

Now take turns reading this lesson's article aloud, switching readers with each paragraph. Then discuss the questions at the end of the article.

Lesson

ARTICLE

GOD WILL COMPLETE WHAT HE STARTED

5 MINUTES

The Philippian church was made up of individuals who would probably never be partners in anything if it were left up to them. But Christ's saving work tore down every barrier that existed among them. Jesus united each one not only to himself but also to one another. This is a union not based on social commonalities, but on the truths of the gospel. Together, they are caught up in a divine fellowship: partakers in the gospel, and partners with Paul in the great mission of God.

When speaking of partnership in verse 5, Paul uses the well-known Greek word *koinonia*. In the New Testament, it always refers to a two-sided relationship where there is a shared identity because of the gospel of Christ Jesus. This is what evokes joy as Paul prays for the Philippians. Partnership in this case is defined not only by a shared goal (although that is important) but more significantly by relationship. Paul and the Philippians belong to God and each other. They are caught up in a belonging that God has created and sustains.

This makes Paul confident for them. What God has started *in them*, God will complete *in them*. There is no doubt! God comes to his people, opens their eyes, gives faith to believe, and draws them to himself. And then God makes sure that nothing—not suffering, not their own sin, not the sin of others against them—ever separates them from his love again.* God ensures that his work will be completed.

Through gospel faith, this word is for us too. No matter what our individual backgrounds before Christ, we can proclaim together that we are hopeless in our sin apart from the saving work of Jesus, and that we are now joined with God on his gospel mission. Yes, our sin and suffering tempt us to think God may have stepped away. As fickle people, we often start things and then give up. But God does not! While his work in us is not yet complete (and will not be complete until the day of Jesus Christ when he returns, or when we go to be with him), God has indeed begun a good work in us. Right now, God is working in us.

And since God is working, we can be sure that he will finish what he started in us. That means each of us can say, "God started a good work in *me*. I am not alone. Even when I struggle, he does not leave me. He will not give up on me. And he will keep me safe until I see him." Just as Christ initially came and died for us while we were still sinners, he continues to come to us and work in us. We are firmly in the grip of his grace. *That* is worth rejoicing about.

I want to be honest with you: I often forget this truth. My belief slips into unbelief, and when that happens my life starts to feel very different. My focus shifts from what *God* has done and is doing to what I think *I* should be doing. I wonder if I am doing enough for God, so I begin making resolution after resolution. My burdens mount. But when nothing is enough and my failure overwhelms me, it dawns on me that my joy in Christ Jesus has completely disappeared. Where did my joy go? It left with my faith! I have forgotten to believe the gospel for me!

---

* See Romans 8:35–39.

I need to run back to Jesus and see that he has paid it all for me. I must remember and believe that God began a good work in me and God will complete his good work. He will bring it all the way to completion, on his good timeline. He is not worried about where I am at this moment. I am not alone, and it is not up to me. Because of Jesus Christ, God has taken hold of me. As I begin to believe afresh these truths of the gospel, my heart revives and my mind clears. As I begin trusting again in what Jesus has done, I stop trusting what I can do, and again I am filled with joy.

When we find ourselves without joy, we need to remember that we have a Father and that he has begun a good work in us. He will work in us to make us who he says we are, and we will partner with him in that. We really can rest in the finished work of Christ on our behalf—a work that has never depended on our faithfulness, but only on the faithfulness of God. We might be failing, falling, kicking, or screaming, but nothing will keep God from completing his process in us and bringing us to eternal joy.

Like Paul, we need to believe and proclaim this truth in the middle of our prison. We might not be in a literal prison, but we all know what it is like to be in the midst of hardship or feel stuck in our circumstances. Our jail could be sickness, habitual sin, or a toxic relationship. It could be an unmet desire for a spouse or children or a job or family situation that feels impossible. Like Paul, let's not be in denial about our sin and suffering. But at the same time, no matter what, let's have hope in the midst of it.

What is our hope? That we will find our own way out or our own way of overcoming? Certainly not. God pursued us and found us when we were far from him. And wherever we are, whatever our struggle, God is still the one who carries us. God is at work even if it is difficult for us to see. The truth is that God's purposes for our lives will be realized. God will complete what he has begun.

DISCUSSION *10 MINUTES*

What "prisons" or struggles tend to make you wonder if God has stepped away from his work in you?

Like the author, have you shifted between thinking you must make resolutions *for* God and remembering that you partner *with* God as he works in you? What does the difference look like in your life?

GOD'S PAST AND FUTURE FAITHFULNESS

20 MINUTES

If you are a believer saved through faith in Jesus, that whole salvation from first to last is a work of God. It was God who first opened your heart to believe the gospel, and who counted you forever righteous instead of guilty because Jesus died for your sin (we call that *justification*). From that day on, it is God who continues to work in you to help your love increase and to make you more holy (we call that *sanctification*). And going forward, it is God who will one day give you a resurrection body and free you from all sin both in the world around you and inside of you (we call that *glorification*). What God began, he will complete.

For this exercise, you'll create some prayer items for your life based on that start-to-finish perspective. On your own, read the prompts below and think of three specific ways God is at work in you: (1) something to thank him for that he's already done, (2) something to pray about that he is doing, and (3) something to ask for that you hope he will do. Your purpose is to be encouraged in your current struggles and prayers by seeing God's past and future faithfulness to you. Be prepared to share some of your prayer items with the group at the end of the exercise. (If you aren't yet a believer, or aren't sure, adjust the exercise to consider how you think God has called, is calling, and perhaps will call you to himself.)

WHAT GOD HAS BEGUN. How might you thank God, as Paul did in our passage, for his work already in your life to change you in some specific way? Choose from the following:

- Some way God changed you when you were first converted to make you more like Jesus

- A specific way God has helped your love for him or for certain other people increase since you became a believer

- A way God has used you to advance the mission of his kingdom

I can thank God for _____

_____

_____

WHAT GOD IS DOING. What current challenges can you take to God, with a focus on how God is continuing to work in you today? Choose from the following:

- A current condition of your heart or circumstance of life that feels like a "prison," but could be a setting for God to increase your faith or holiness

- Some specific way God is teaching you to grow in your love for him or for certain other people you are regularly challenged to love

- A current struggle or opportunity you face in your work to advance Christ's kingdom

I need to draw near to God today because of _____

_____

_____

WHAT YOU HOPE GOD WILL DO. How might you pray, in a way similar to Paul, for God to continue his work in you going forward? Choose from the following:

- Some aspect of the person you surely will be in the next age, when God's work to make you like Jesus is complete and the struggle you have with a certain sin is finally over
- A specific way you see yourself being able to better love God or certain other people
- A way God might be calling you to greater service for the mission of his kingdom

I can ask God to work in his time to make me _____

_____

_____

When the group is ready, share some of your prayer items. What has God done in you, what is he doing, and what do you hope he will do? How does looking at God's past or future work in you encourage you in your present struggles?

WRAP-UP AND PRAYER *10 MINUTES*

Pray together for God's work in each of you. Make the wishes Paul mentions in his prayer, and the prayer items you came up with in the exercise, a model for what you pray together.

3

SUFFERING

BIG IDEA

Even as we experience trouble, our hearts can respond in joy because of the gospel.

BIBLE CONVERSATION *20 MINUTES*

Remember that the backdrop for Paul's letter is that he wrote it from prison. Although he had done nothing wrong in preaching about Jesus, his situation was serious. His accusers wanted to end his ministry by ending his life. They falsely claimed he had caused riots and profaned the temple and were asking the Romans to sentence him to die.* Paul was dearly hoping to be able to continue his missionary journeys and visit Philippi again, but he did not know whether he would be released, kept in prison, or executed. Amid this personal uncertainty, his letter gives us insight into how to deal with suffering.

Have someone read **Philippians 1:12–30**, or have a few readers take turns. Then discuss the questions below:

---

* See Acts 24:5–6; 25:7–11; 26:31–32.

List some outcomes that matter more to Paul than whether he lives or dies. Which of those desires most impresses you, and why?

How is Paul's joy like your joy or different from it? Explain.

Why is it important to Paul that the Philippians keep "standing firm in one spirit (v. 27)," and how might that instruction benefit the church today?

****

Now read the article from this book's author. Take turns reading aloud by paragraph, and discuss the questions that follow when you finish.

JOY IN THE MIDST OF STRUGGLE

5 MINUTES

I want to ask you an impolite question. When you think about your life, what do you think needs to happen for you to have joy today? What situation in your life stands between you and contentment?

Oh, you might say, *If I just had more money, I would be happy. If my grades were better, I would be happy. If my husband would only stop being such a jerk, I would be happy. I could be happy if I could finally find a spouse. I would be happy if this person would stop saying wrong things about me. I could have joy if I had a different roommate. I need my kids to give their hearts to Jesus.* The list goes on and on and on.

In the days leading up to his crucifixion and after his resurrection, Jesus promised to always be with us and to give us peace. But he also said something we often do not want to hear: "In the world you will have tribulation" (John 16:33). Suffering, it seems, is also a promise Jesus made to us.

While we do not like this promise, our hearts know it's true. Believers undergo very difficult trials. We are not the only ones who suffer, but being a Christian does not mean life is free of trouble. And sometimes, as was the case with Paul, being a Christian is actually what brings the trouble. Jesus told his disciples to count the cost.* He was preparing them for the reality that life in this world, even (or especially) as a Christian, is not always easy. Sometimes we do the right thing and people do not like it. Sometimes we talk about Christ and people do not like it.

Even though we understand this intellectually, we can still struggle to accept it when we or someone we love is in the midst of a painful trial. Our resistance to accepting suffering is not unique to our generation or culture. Here in this part of Philippians, Paul himself is writing from a place of hardship—prison! As we hear him talk about his struggle, we get to see how he responded to the suffering in his life and how he exhorts the Philippians to respond.

Paul wants the Philippians to know that, even though it appears that from jail he can no longer work as a missionary and start new churches, he trusts that God is still using him. He proclaims, "What has happened to me has really served to advance the gospel" (v. 12). Paul rejoices even in jail because he believes that God is still pushing the gospel forward.

Do you see what a strange viewpoint this is? Paul is not saying, "I have failed." He is not saying, "I was so important for the spread of the gospel, and now it is all over because I am in prison." Paul is not looking for someone to blame or wondering what he could have done differently to avoid prison. Even in a desperate situation, Paul says, "I rejoice" and "I will continue to rejoice." He looks forward and hopes to be released, but his joy does not depend on such a release happening.

Rejoice is not a word we tend to use on a daily basis. Perhaps that's because we think it involves acting like the suffering is not difficult. But why does Paul rejoice? Is he telling us that being in a Roman jail

---

*See Luke 14:26–33.

is not challenging? That he is fine with his present circumstances? Not in the least! Instead, Paul can rejoice because he knows that despite his suffering there is something *more* true about him that even the cruelest guards cannot touch.

Paul knows who he is in Christ. He knows that God will work for his good and for the gospel. Whether he is free or in jail, whether he lives or dies, the focus of Paul's life is on his Lord and Savior Jesus Christ. And because of that, his heart is free.

Paul would be very happy to be out of jail. And I would love for your grades to go well, for your husband to straighten up, or for you to have a good boss and more money. But whether or not those things happen, you can have joy because of Christ. Through his coming, living, dying, and rising for you, your peace does not depend on your circumstances. Remember that you are eternally safe in him and he is working all things for your good, in love. That will free your heart.

When our difficult circumstances do not improve despite all our efforts, it is easy to become discouraged or even believe God has abandoned us there. In fact, there was a time when Jesus's own circumstances looked pretty bleak. He experienced all the trouble this world could dole out. But because he pressed on and submitted to his Father, he gained the victory—not just for himself but also for us.

You see, when Jesus promised suffering, he didn't end there. When he said, "In the world you will have tribulation" he followed that up with, "But take heart; I have overcome the world." As Paul will tell us later in Philippians 4:6, in Christ it is possible to have peace that transcends our understanding of how our lives are going. Christ has promised that, and Paul believes it. Even in prison, without knowing whether he will live or die, Paul can say, "I rejoice." Like him, we too can look around at whatever our prison is and trust that God's purposes for us will prevail, because Christ has overcome the world. And from that, we too can rejoice.

DISCUSSION *10 MINUTES*

What situations in your life feel like they stand between you and joy?

How do you react to Jesus's encouragement that he has overcome the world? What makes it helpful amid your suffering, or leaves things still difficult? Explain.

Lesson

3

EXERCISE

A GOSPEL MANNER OF LIFE

20 MINUTES

In the last part of our passage, Paul tells the Philippians how to respond to his situation: "Only let your manner of life be worthy of the gospel of Christ" (v. 27). This means more than just trying to be good. The Greek wording suggests the mannerisms of a citizen. As a believer, you have a particular way of acting because of who you are and the customs of your homeland—heaven. As suffering draws out the real you, you respond like someone whose home is with Jesus.

On your own, read about the differences between a worldly manner of life and a gospel manner, based on Paul's explanations in our passage. Notice some customs that fit your life—both ways you still act like a citizen of the world and ways you have learned to act like the citizen of heaven you are. Be ready to discuss your findings at the end of the exercise.

SELF-PROTECTION vs. UNITY

"Standing firm in one spirit, with one mind striving side by side for the faith of the gospel . . ." (v. 27).

Worldly Manner	Gospel Manner
Faced with suffering, scarcity, or tough decisions, I get protective of myself and demanding about what I think is best. My me-first or I'm-right instincts kick in.	I remember that in Christ I am rich in the heavenly treasures that matter most. I rest in the can't-lose-it love of my Father, who provides all I need in this life and a rich inheritance in the next.
I may become jealous of others who avoid pain I must endure. I may use gossip or manipulation to get ahead or advance what's "right."	Knowing that Christ provides and protects makes me able to be generous and accept being last. I am teachable and submit to godly leaders.
I jump to blame people when things go wrong.	I'm understanding when things go wrong.
Convinced that the times are scary, I'm angry with anyone who gets in my way or takes an approach I think is wrong.	Convinced that Christ reigns, I stand with fellow believers to honor and trust him, rather than opposing them to win my preferences.

FEAR vs. CONFIDENCE

". . . and not frightened in anything by your opponents. This is a clear sign to them of their destruction, but of your salvation, and that from God" (v. 28).

Worldly Manner	Gospel Manner
Faced with the prospect of suffering, I make decisions out of fear.	I make decisions out of confidence in Christ.
I worry about harm or failure, so I avoid risk, or I become willing to cheat or harm others to keep myself from failing.	In the end, I know Christ will not fail and his plans will not suffer harm, so I can be aboveboard and kind in whatever I do.
I worry about disgrace or discomfort, so I become willing to lie or shift blame.	In the end and in Christ, no disgrace will stick to me, so I can always be honest.
I feel that my survival and my reputation depend on me, and the result is anxiety or even a lingering sense of dread. Uncertainty gnaws at me.	I may be uncertain what will happen on the way, but I am sure my end is not destruction. This frees me from worry and selfishness, and lets me love others.

AVOIDANCE vs. WILLINGNESS

"For it has been granted to you that for the sake of Christ you should not only believe in him but also suffer for his sake, engaged in the same conflict" (vv. 29–30).

Worldly Manner	Gospel Manner
The avoidance of suffering or discomfort guides my life. I help others based on my skills or my excess rather than their needs.	I see the big pattern of life: that like my Savior, I endure suffering and discomfort now that surely will lead to victory.
I get annoyed when I'm asked for something that will be a bother.	I see the glory in dying to my me-first reflexes—starting in small, everyday ways.
I resist ministry opportunities or acts of kindness that are outside my comfort zone, explaining how they are "not my calling."	My calling is to serve Christ, even in discomfort or suffering, which welds me all the more to him.
My ministry involvement feels more like a hobby than like I'm part of the eternal conflict between evil and the gospel, where injuries are part of the fight.	Jesus will twist evil for my good and the glory of his kingdom. So I am willing to engage his mission even when that means entering darkness, knowing hurt, or confronting evil.

When the group is ready, discuss what you noticed. How has God taught you to live in a gospel manner, and how do you want to grow so that your customs better fit your home with Christ?

WRAP-UP AND PRAYER *10 MINUTES*

Prayer is a key part of a gospel manner. All of your salvation, including your progress in living like a citizen of heaven, is "from God" (v. 28). So pray together that your Father will deliver you from evil, be near you in suffering, and teach you his customs.

Lesson

4

HUMILITY

BIG IDEA

When Christ takes hold of our lives, he enables us to lay down our lives so others can know him.

BIBLE CONVERSATION *20 MINUTES*

So far in his letter to the Philippians, Paul has emphasized how the finished work of Christ (1) gives us a new identity in him, (2) also unites us to each other in him, and (3) makes us all side-by-side partners in God's mission to the world. For Paul, Christian community and mission are not add-ons chosen by some believers, but an essential part of the Christian life for all believers. Now in the second chapter of his letter, he will urge us to live out that life fully.

The passage will end with a poetic-sounding section that Paul structures around two broad truths about Jesus. The first is Christ's *humiliation*: how he made himself low, coming to us as a man and dying for us. The second is Christ's *exaltation*: how he rose, ascended to reign in heaven and send the Holy Spirit, and will return in glory. With this structure in mind, have someone read **Philippians 2:1–11** aloud. Then discuss these questions:

How is the Christian community described in verses 1–5 different from communities you've experienced?

Look at the details Paul mentions when writing about Jesus's humility in verses 6–8. Are there things about Jesus you've seldom considered before, or elements that stand out to you? Explain.

What about Jesus's exaltation described in verses 9–11 is new or note-worthy to you, and why?

✳✳✳✳

Next, read this lesson's article. Take turns reading aloud by paragraph. Then discuss the questions that follow.

THE MIND OF CHRIST

5 MINUTES

At the start of chapter 2, Paul presents four gospel pillars. There's a progression in these: (1) Foundationally, we have "encouragement in Christ," united to him forever by faith and receiving all he has done for us by his living and dying and rising. (2) We have "comfort from love," realizing that God's motivation for sending Christ to do all of this was his unshakable love for us. (3) We have "participation in the Spirit," God's actual presence and power and comfort in us. (4) We therefore rest in the assurance that we enjoy God's "affection and sympathy" every day and on into eternity.

With these gospel pillars in place, Paul is ready to make his plea. If indeed we have experienced God in these ways—and Paul expects us to say that of course we have—then it should change the way we interact with one another. Jesus said our love would be a signpost to the kingdom of God: "By this all people will know that you are my disciples, if you have love for one another" (John 13:35). Love and unity and humility are other-worldly behaviors that point to our identity in Christ and our new citizenship in heaven.

Paul knows that on this side of heaven, we will never practice these perfectly and that there can be real struggles in a church or ministry. In fact, the more these gospel pillars move us to live out our faith with other people, the more our need for the gospel is exposed. Why? Pride. Or as this passage puts it, selfish ambition and conceit. If we live and do ministry with other humans, it won't take long for selfishness to bubble up.

But together, we can keep running back to Jesus and remembering that we are helpless to change without him. The good news is that we will always find our Father willing to abundantly pour out his mercy on us. He is no longer angry with us, because all of his wrath was poured out on Christ on the cross. As he restores us, we are again filled with fresh faith that expresses itself in love for those around us.

This dynamic is how we both grow and go. God has a mission in the world to draw people to himself. As we experience God's love, it launches us into that mission. The gospel pushes us into the world to proclaim and demonstrate Christ, loving other people. And it pushes us as believers into the world *together*, loving each other as a witness.

However, when we're trying to love people and live humbly with each other, we find it is difficult. If you're like me, you don't even have to go into the world; all you have to do is spend some time with the other people in your own house and you will have difficulties. The gospel's fullness in us starts to leak. We forget how needy we are and how much Christ has done for us. We become prideful or discouraged. We might have great affection for those who are on mission with us, but if we spend enough time together we will eventually find something to argue about.

These are opportunities for us to repent, humble ourselves, and go back and find Christ again. Being on mission helps us see our need to do this daily. We learn to confess our sins and enjoy the forgiveness and perfect righteousness Christ gives. And when we encounter his love and grace for us in this ongoing way, it fuels us again to love those around us. Then as we interact with others, we again see the limits of our love and have to run again to Jesus. For Paul, this is how the

Christian life is lived. As we increasingly know Christ, he pushes us into the mission of God. And as we engage with others in mission, we find we need Christ all the more. Jesus grows large for us.

Paul says that in Christ Jesus, we have the mind of Christ. What a remarkable statement! Part of what this means is that, because of all Christ has accomplished for us, we can now enter into Jesus's own story of laying down his life for us. Paul launches into a great poem that tells that story. It is *the* story that both propels us into mission in the first place and restores us when mission is hard and our humility fails.

The first thing Paul says is that Christ emptied himself of what was rightfully his by taking the form of a servant. Remember how Paul started the letter: "Paul and Timothy, servants of Christ Jesus." Paul describes himself as a servant because the Lord he loves became a servant. When we follow the exhortation to value others above ourselves, it puts us right into Jesus's own story.

But that story is about an upside-down kingdom, because when Christ humbled himself even to the point of death, what did God do? God raised him up. And by faith, as we too humble ourselves and lay down our lives for others, we can trust that God will raise us up along with Jesus. That raising up may occur in this life or it may happen in the life to come. But we can trust that because we are in Christ, we are grafted into his resurrection story.

As believers, we hold onto the promise that when we lose our lives for Christ we find our purpose in the world. Jesus said, "Whoever loses his life for my sake will find it" (Matthew 16:25). We give up our lives as a way of pointing to the one who, when he gave up his life for us, brought us from death to life in him. So, in his name, we build loving, unified, gracious, missional, and sacrificial communities. While these communities are not perfect, they are so counter to this world's operating principles that people cannot help but notice.

DISCUSSION *10 MINUTES*

What might be some ways for your group of believers to encourage each other to be humble and to practice this together within your group?

Humility requires staying close to Jesus and being refreshed with his story. How might you, as a group, also encourage each other to do that?

EXERCISE

4

JESUS'S STORY AND YOUR STORY
20 MINUTES

A big part of understanding how Jesus humbled himself for you and was exalted for you is that it means you no longer have to pretend. You don't have to hide from the world or other believers, acting like you're better than you really are. It's okay for people to see that you struggle and fail and often fall into sin, because you have a Savior who died and rose for that kind of person. You can take your problems to Christ, and also take others to him with you.

On your own, think about how your connection to Jesus's down-and-up life matters when your own Christian life gets difficult. Work through each step of the exercise below, and be ready to discuss some of your responses.

STEP 1: JESUS'S STORY. Begin by reminding yourself of the gospel's meaning for you if you have believed, as seen in Jesus's humiliation and exaltation. Here's a summary:

- **Humiliation: Jesus became a human** and came to earth on a mission to save you. He knows the weaknesses and troubles of human life in this world, and has been tempted in every way you are, and sympathizes (Hebrews 4:15).

- **Humiliation: Jesus suffered and died** on the cross in your place. Unlike you, he obeyed God perfectly, and then he took on himself the curse and shame and punishment for all your sin. He credits you with his perfectly righteous record, and you are a dearly loved child of God (Galatians 3:13; 2 Corinthians 5:21).

- **Turning Point: Jesus went to the grave and came out alive.** In him, you are dead to sin and are spiritually alive, able to be godly and to offer your own life in thanksgiving (Romans 6:4–14). He allowed himself to become a corpse so that you might not fear death but would know he has power over it and will raise you too from the grave to glory (Hebrews 2:14–15).

- **Exaltation: Jesus ascended to heaven** to reign and to constantly help you. From your own future home, he sends the Holy Spirit to comfort you, to build your desire for heavenly things, and to provide you with his above-every-name power as you go on mission. He continually joins his prayer with yours as you ask for daily forgiveness and help in living for God (Hebrews 7:24–25).

- **Exaltation: Jesus will return in glory** to vindicate you and destroy evil. The same person who lovingly died to take your punishment will be the Judge who declares you spotless and brings you into perfect life with him (Matthew 25:34). He will condemn all of his and your enemies, crush sin and death forever, and remake the world into a home where God's glory is forever known and enjoyed.

STEP 2: YOUR STORY. How is it hard for you to love others and live humbly on mission? Think of an incident in your life, which you can tell the group about, that fits <u>one</u> of the following conditions:

Disinterest. Think of a time you failed to see the point of living humbly or on mission, or to be excited about an opportunity to do so. You needed the gospel to energize you to go out.

Cold-heartedness. Think of a time you protected yourself or held back because you didn't care enough about people to live humbly or join in mission. You needed the gospel to awaken your love for Jesus and others.

Disappointment. Think of a time you *were* trying to live humbly or participate in ministry/mission, but the results were discouraging. Your disappointment was prodding you to draw closer to Jesus to be refreshed and renewed.

Condemnation. Think of a time you *were* trying to live humbly or participate in ministry/mission, but you failed in a way that felt personally condemning. Your obvious need for Jesus was pressing you to discover more deeply his love for you.

The time in my life that I'm thinking of is: _____

_____.

STEP 3: MATCH JESUS'S STORY WITH YOURS. The whole story of Jesus, both his humiliation and his exaltation, meets you when your Christian life is hard. Consider the hard time you mentioned above, and be ready to answer one of the following questions:

1. What parts of Jesus's story motivated you to start loving others or go on mission, or what might motivate you in a similar situation now? (Try to find something in *both* Jesus's humiliation and his exaltation that moves you toward love/mission.)

2. What parts of Jesus's story became more meaningful to you when loving others or being on mission got difficult, or what

might do so? (Try to find something in *both* Jesus's humiliation and his exaltation that help when you're disappointed or have failed.)

When the group is ready, share and explain your answers. How does Jesus's story motivate yours, and how does your story drive you back to his?

WRAP-UP AND PRAYER *10 MINUTES*

In your prayer time together, ask God to make you more like Christ, especially in his humility.

Lesson

5

MISSION

BIG IDEA

In the midst of our struggles, God makes us shine like stars in a dark world.

BIBLE CONVERSATION *20 MINUTES*

In the previous passage (Philippians 2:1–11), Paul has just finished a poem about Christ's humiliation-to-exaltation conquest. In this passage, he will follow that by urging the Philippians, "Work out your own salvation with fear and trembling." He does not mean Jesus's saving conquest over sin is somehow insufficient, as if we needed to worriedly provide some missing piece on our end. But part of Christ's all-inclusive salvation is that we become more holy, and, in this part, we cooperate. In fact, we do so with no-nonsense diligence precisely because we know how thoroughly Jesus opposes sin and how God himself is already at work in us to break sin.

This effort to be Christlike will show up in service and mission. In addition to himself and his travel companion Timothy, Paul will mention a missionary named Epaphroditus whom the Philippians sent to him with gifts to see to his needs while in prison (see 4:18). We know nothing about Epaphroditus beyond what's in this letter, where he appears to be one of the many gospel missionaries throughout history who have been sent out in a support role, which Paul includes as part of "the work of Christ."

Have someone read **Philippians 2:12–30** aloud, or have a few readers take turns. Then discuss the following questions:

Look at the wording Paul uses to describe how the Philippians should behave in the world. What does he say that especially encourages you to work at being godly? Explain.

Earlier in verses 4 and 5, Paul said we should have the same unselfish interests and attitudes as Jesus. What do you admire about how Paul, Timothy, or Epaphroditus act like Jesus?

How well do you relate to the obstacles and dangers these three missionaries faced in their service?

* * * *

Next, take turns reading the article aloud, switching readers with each paragraph. Then discuss the questions at the end of the article.

5

SHINING LIKE STARS

5 MINUTES

Years ago, I traveled with my friend Hunter to Siberia for a month. We had been invited to come teach and encourage some of the pastors and ministry teams there. We finally made it to a layover with a local missionary only to be awakened in the middle of the night and told that to reach our next destination city, we had to hurry. We needed to get to a bus stop two miles away, and we each needed to carry a backpack with fifty pounds of books. We were a sight to be seen—four o'clock in the morning, no breakfast, jetlagged, nine flights of stairs, running two miles to the bus station in thirty degrees below zero. And we missed the bus. It was not our best moment.

But there was more. From the bus stop, we hiked another mile to the missionary's office where we met our translator, Nelly. While she cooked us some breakfast, I was eclipsed by fatigue and I suddenly fainted. Hunter put out his arm and caught me on the way down. When Nelly turned to see what had happened, she found Hunter and me in what looked like a graceful dance move—a dip—just as I woke up. We turned and looked at Nelly. She quickly spun back around toward the stove. It was all very awkward. We never spoke about it afterward.

Despite this beginning, our trip was amazing. God helped us encourage the local churches with the good news of his grace. What's more, we got to see the amazing work they were doing to build God's kingdom in such a seemingly-forsaken place. If you had told me on that first morning that our time in Siberia would be such a rich time of ministry, I would have said you were crazy. But this is what God does as Christ takes hold of us and makes us his partners in the gospel. God really has chosen the weak and foolish things of this world—like me, like you—to be his witnesses in spite of our awkwardness and failures.

In Philippians, Paul has given us a vision for what life and ministry can be like as we live out the Jesus story together as citizens of heaven. It's such a hopeful vision! So why is it so hard to hold on to? Well, like Hunter and I experienced at the beginning of our Siberian journey, we have a hard time outrunning our own neediness.

Reminders of our neediness might be physical, like exhaustion or a bad back. They might be emotional, like attending another baby shower when you long to have your own child. They might be relational, like when your husband says he has to work late—again. They might be behavioral, like when you sinned again in the same destructive way even though you long to stop. Each time, you hear a faint whisper that makes you wonder if God has abandoned you. In those moments, it is very hard to trust in God's love for you, much less that you have anything to give to his mission.

Our instinct is often to believe that once the challenge or unmet need we are facing has been resolved, then we can get about the business of laying down our lives for the sake of the kingdom. However, God doesn't save us and make us perfect right away. He leaves us here and calls us to obedience. We work for his kingdom even *while* we remain dependent on him, feeling our humanness all the time and having to rely on his righteousness.

In this passage, Paul seems to acknowledge this tension. If it were easy to live out of faith all the time, it would not be something we need to work out. But this side of heaven, too often we still forget the gospel and resort to trying to earn our own righteousness. On a daily-life level, we use other things besides Christ to meet our needs. To overcome this, we need to take hold of Christ who laid hold of us. We need to work *out* what he has worked *in* us.

How does this look on a daily basis? Faith expresses itself by moving toward other people in love, even when we are needy. That is working out our salvation with fear and trembling. We walk by faith, trusting that God is working to fulfill his good purpose even if we do not understand how. We hold firmly to the word of life, which is the gospel of Jesus, knowing that God loves us and will take care of us in this situation. He is not asleep. He has not forgotten. Can we believe that? God is at work in our lives, and he is crazy about us.

Paul draws our attention to an ordinary behavior that might indicate we have left the gospel in the rearview mirror: grumbling and complaining. This recalls the grumbling of the Israelites in their wilderness wanderings. We may empathize. Their journey was long, there was no water, and they had to eat strange food. But it did not take long before those hardships led them to doubt that their Deliverer had their best interests at heart: "Is the LORD among us or not?" (Exodus 17:7).

But God did deliver those people. And now Paul says we should not spend time grumbling and doubting. Instead, trust in God will make us look different from the crooked generation around us. We will shine like stars. You know, sometimes I struggle with a problem or a sin in my life, and progress seems horribly slow. But God's work in us guarantees we *will* make progress. And while we work through our neediness, we become lights in the world. By God's power, in the midst of a messy and incomplete here and now, he makes us shine like stars in the darkness.

DISCUSSION *10 MINUTES*

What was a time when, in your service to Christ, you felt nothing like a shining star—but God used you despite your own neediness?

What kinds of situations might cause you to wonder, *Is the Lord among us or not?*

Lesson

5

EXERCISE

MISSION FEARS
20 MINUTES

Whether your way to participate in God's mission seems big or little, and whether it takes you around the world or just next door, you will have fears about it. For this exercise, think about how God may be calling you to mission and what you fear about it, or why you resist it. On your own, read through the list of possible fears below. Assign each a rating from 1 to 5, with 1 meaning you don't have that fear at all and 5 meaning it's a big cause of resistance for you. Then answer some questions about how the gospel addresses your fear, and be ready to discuss with the group.

☐ 5
☐ 4   **Sickness or death.** I fear that what happened to Paul or
☐ 3   Epaphroditus might happen to me or my family, or that mission
☐ 2   might compromise our health and safety.
☐ 1

☐ 5
☐ 4   **Deprivation.** I fear that, like the Israelites, I or my family might face
☐ 3   shortages of basic needs or comforts I'm used to having.
☐ 2
☐ 1

☐ 5
☐ 4   **Failure.** I fear being exposed as a washout or viewed as
☐ 3   incompetent, or revealed to have nothing to give to God's mission
☐ 2   or even harmful to it.
☐ 1

48

☐ 5
☐ 4
☐ 3
☐ 2
☐ 1

Neediness. I fear having to become dependent on others like Paul was, or more obviously dependent on God, asking for help, unable to feel confident about meeting my own needs.

☐ 5
☐ 4
☐ 3
☐ 2
☐ 1

Embarrassment. I fear being culturally or socially awkward or uncomfortable, looking out of place, or taking foolish missteps.

☐ 5
☐ 4
☐ 3
☐ 2
☐ 1

Uncertainty. I fear possibly making the wrong decision about mission, or living with many unknowns for me and my family.

☐ 5
☐ 4
☐ 3
☐ 2
☐ 1

Spiritual demands. I fear/resist having my sin exposed, or having it bubble up so that I have to step up my efforts at personal holiness and remaining close to God.

☐ 5
☐ 4
☐ 3
☐ 2
☐ 1

Emotional struggles. I fear loneliness, potential stress in relationships, reminders of hurts in my life, or other emotional hardships that might accompany mission.

☐ 5
☐ 4
☐ 3
☐ 2
☐ 1

Opposition. I fear being disliked or belittled because of my commitment to Jesus, or making someone angry with me, critical of me, or disappointed with me—perhaps even friends or certain members of my own family.

☐ 5
☐ 4
☐ 3
☐ 2
☐ 1

Other: _____

_____

Paul has already said in Philippians 1:27–30 that you should not be afraid to engage in the cause of Christ and suffer for him, because (1) your salvation is sure and is from God and (2) you are standing firm together with others. Pick one of your highest-rated fears and briefly answer the following questions:

How does the salvation you have in Jesus address your fear? _____

_____

_____

How might you involve others as you pursue Jesus and mission? ___

_____

_____

_____

When the group is ready, share some of your responses. Why do you resist stepping out to love others and serve God's mission, and what encourages you amid those needs?

WRAP-UP AND PRAYER *10 MINUTES*

As a part of your prayer time, you might pray for missionaries you know and for your own opportunities to tell about Christ and serve his kingdom.

Lesson

6

JOY

BIG IDEA

It is total garbage to try to earn a righteous record before God, but receiving the righteousness of Christ by faith leads to joy.

BIBLE CONVERSATION *20 MINUTES*

In Philippians 3 we get to the centerpiece of what Paul is saying to his Philippian friends, and what evokes the most joy for him: imputed righteousness. While every other religion is about what humans must do to satisfy God or earn some heavenly life, the gospel puts all the qualifying work onto God himself.

- Only Jesus, the Son of God, lived the truly righteous life God requires. Only Jesus did not deserve to die.

- But Jesus took the full punishment for sin that we deserve, in our place. In return, he credits us with—or *imputes* to us—his own righteous record.

- We become joined to him this way by faith alone. His righteous record is a pure gift to us, not earned by any good works we do or sincerity we muster up, but received as we believe he is the Savior and trust him to be our Savior.

- This means we enter life with God, and remain there, because we possess Jesus's righteousness instead of by any good works we do. Whatever good we do ourselves flows from the fact that Jesus has already brought us into life with God.

Paul will use himself as the prime example of how religious performance can't save us and might actually keep us from trusting Christ if we trust it instead. Paul will mention how he was once a **Pharisee**. Pharisees were highly-committed Jews admired for studying and strictly obeying God's law, and Paul had been trained by one of their most celebrated teachers.* Paul will also refer to **Judaizers**, whom he calls evildoers. The Judaizers were false teachers in the church who claimed that in addition to faith in Christ, believers must obey parts of the Old Testament ceremonial law that pointed forward to Christ, including being circumcised. And Paul will denounce confidence in the **flesh**. He's condemning the Judaizers who trusted in being circumcised, but for Paul, the flesh also means any self-based behavior.

Now have someone read **Philippians 3:1–11** aloud. Then discuss the questions below:

Explain why Paul uses such strong language when he writes about the Judaizers. What does he feel is so wrong about their devotion to the Jewish way?

---

* See Acts 22:3.

Look at Paul's list of his own credentials that might make him feel right with God. How does it compare to things that might make you feel you've earned a right standing with God?

According to Paul, what attitudes result when you receive a righteous record from God? How are they different from attitudes you might have if you think your own credentials make you right with God?

．

****

Now take turns reading this lesson's article, switching readers at each paragraph break. Then discuss the questions at the end of the article.

Lesson

ARTICLE

THE RIGHTEOUSNESS OF CHRIST

5 MINUTES

When I first came to Christ I was in my last year of high school. Everywhere I went from that point on, I carried a big Bible and a pocket full of the evangelism pamphlets titled *Have You Heard of the Four Spiritual Laws?* I would talk to anybody about Jesus. We had seven minutes between classes, so I figured I could take one minute to find someone and four minutes to cover the *Four Spiritual Laws*, and I would still have two minutes to get to my next class. I was happy and dangerous.

One day my cousin Susan marched up to me in the hallway and blurted out, "Josiah, you have to stop this! We have the same last name, and I can't get a date because of you. What are you saying all the time, anyway?" I saw my opportunity and got out the *Four Spiritual Laws*. As I started to explain, she got so angry she was jumping up and down. But before she stormed off, I slid the pamphlet into her purse. Three months later, she came to me and said, "Last night I read it, and I received Christ." Today she is a pastor's wife and her testimony continues. God used my foolishness.

I continued to be excited about Jesus, and he used me in unusual ways. I went to seminary. I became a pastor. I started new churches. I knew much and worked hard. I studied, and God used Barbara and me to bring people to Christ. We were sending missionaries out from our church, and we saw many people grow in their faith. However, over those years I lost something. I lost my original joy. It would sometimes come back a little, but then I would lose it again.

You see, we can know about joy in our head, formally, and not have joy in our heart, practically. I might believe in Christ intellectually, but practically I put confidence in myself—even to do good things, keep God's law, and work in ministry. That's what was happening. I was trying to do God's will in my own strength.

And this was hidden from me because the flesh blinds us. Jesus said to Pharisees like Paul that their self-trust blinded them.* If you had said to me, "Josiah, you're trusting yourself and not God," I would have said, "No, that's not right. I pray a lot," because my flesh blinded me to what I was actually trusting. When I try to use God's law in a wrong way, or when I try to pursue Christ in my own efforts, or when I try to minister out of my own ability, there is a consequence. All that effort blinds me to what my heart is actually doing, and I lose my joy.

So, if you can't see your heart, how do you know this is happening? You can work it backward. When you lose the fruit of the Spirit, you can know something is wrong in your heart. Even if you can't see it directly, you can tell by the loss of love, joy, peace, patience, and so on. When that fruit of the Spirit begins to leave your life, you can know you are trusting something other than Jesus.

Paul had the right heritage and a perfect record according to Jewish law, but there was a problem with his heart that did not show up in his list of external law-keeping. If we read the book of Acts, we see that

* See John 9:39–41.

Paul was an angry man. His righteousness was so based in himself that he was "breathing threats and murder" (Acts 9:1) and later admitted he'd had "raging fury" (Acts 26:11). From other people's viewpoints, he was blameless. But inside, he was not blameless before God.

When God took hold of Paul's life, Paul realized that his outward righteousness did not impress God. In fact, the righteousness he thought was to his gain he then "counted as loss for the sake of Christ." Paul not only counts these things as loss, he considers them "rubbish" in verse 8, which is literally the word for human excrement. Whenever we work in our own strength, no matter how large or small our efforts are, even our best efforts are worth less than nothing before God. We count them as loss. We see they are rubbish compared to what Christ offers us.

Paul begins his testimony speaking in the past tense, but he quickly brings it forward to the present in verse 8. He is not just talking about when he first became a Christian. This exercise of counting all else loss is something that keeps happening *today*. Paul knows he must daily be vigilant about his flesh's efforts to find its own righteousness. Counting it as loss is an exercise we all need to engage in daily. Doing so helps us see and be astonished by the gospel again and again, so we know the surpassing worth of Christ Jesus.

Perhaps you have never come to Christ before, and today you are ready. How you do that is simple. From your heart, you trust yourself and your best efforts no more. Your best efforts are rubbish. You trust Jesus alone for your relationship with God, not Jesus plus anything else. When you do that the first time, you become a Christian. When you do that every day, you live as a Christian in the joy of the Lord. The way you begin the Christian life is the way you continue the Christian life.

Martin Luther taught that we receive grace like the ground receives rain. What does the ground do? It receives. It does not make the rain.

What does the Christian do? You put aside everything else, and you receive the righteousness of God by faith in Christ. You believe that God is no longer looking in condemnation at all the things you do or do not do. And when you trust that, there is some relief. Joy can start to come. You want to know Christ, and be close to him, and be like him.

DISCUSSION *10 MINUTES*

Has your joy in Christ grown, lessened, or wavered over your Christian life? Why do you think that is?

In your Christian life, what might it look like for you to be like the ground, receiving rain instead of making it rain?

Lesson

EXERCISE

WHERE IS YOUR CONFIDENCE?

20 MINUTES

Your sinful self will naturally look to things other than Christ for your righteousness—the sense that you are all right. To feel right to yourself or to look right to others, you might focus on worldly things (career achievements, family respectability, attractiveness, etc.). But for this exercise, think specifically about *religious things* that make you feel you are right *in God's eyes*. What are you trusting, other than Christ, for your sense that God loves you and is at your side as you serve him?

On your own, work through both steps of the exercise. Be ready to discuss some of your results when you finish.

STEP 1: COUNTERFEIT SOURCES OF RIGHTEOUSNESS. What religious things do you sometimes put your confidence in instead of in Christ? These may be otherwise good things, even evidence of God's work in you that is meant to encourage you. But if you measure God's love for you and his commitment to help you by your performance of them, rather than by Christ's righteousness given to you, they are a "righteousness of your own." Select some that apply to you.

☐ **Heritage or affiliation.** I might sense I am right with God, or not right, based on my church background, correct doctrine, spiritual circle, or devotion to certain celebrated teachers.

☐ **Progress in holiness.** I might sense I am right with God, or not right, based on how quickly I have grown in holy living or the results of my daily battles with certain sins.

☐ **Service to the church.** I might sense I am right with God, or not right, based on my ability to do ministry, help my church, succeed in mission, win converts, act like a Christian, or maintain a passion for these things.

☐ **External rites.** I might sense I am right with God, or not right, based on certain outward decisions, participation, or acts of allegiance I complete.

☐ **Emotional experience.** I might sense I am right with God, or not right, based on a level of sincerity I feel about my faith (my faith is in the quality of my faith instead of in Jesus) or on the degree of affection or fervor I reach during times with God.

☐ **Other:** _____

_____.

STEP 2: CONFIDENCE IN CHRIST. Looking at your own best efforts and credentials will leave you insecure, because only Christ's righteousness is good enough. Paul says a believer will "worship by the Spirit of God and glory in Christ Jesus and put no confidence in the flesh" (v. 3). Even if you know this in your head, you may struggle to live this way daily in your heart. So compare the results of confidence in the flesh—your religious performance—with what results when you put your confidence solely in Christ. Note some ways to want to grow in confidence in Christ.

Results of confidence in the flesh	Results of confidence in Christ
No joy. Living for God feels like a task I must find the strength to complete. I live with a sense of never-can-rest duties, or with self-pride/loathing that comes and goes based on my best-effort record.	**Joy.** I have confidence that Jesus perfectly pleased God on my behalf and will not be thwarted in building his kingdom. I can serve with joy despite sin and setbacks, since my record is not the one that counts.
No love. I am unsure of God's love for me, so I obey him grudgingly to earn his leniency rather than out of love. I have a prove-myself agenda behind my "love" for others, so that I can't genuinely give myself up for them.	**Love.** I have confidence that I'm God's dearly loved child even though my own love is still growing. I can't make God love me more than he already does (he died for me!), which frees me from fake love and makes me a genuine-love junkie.
No peace. Living for God feels like a burden that weighs on me, leaving me with uncertainty that I've done enough. I live with fear or pressure, wondering if I've really convinced God to be on my side.	**Peace.** I have confidence that Jesus made peace with God for me, so that God is not trying to catch me in sin but is on my side. In Christ, I can rest from fear despite ups and downs in my struggle against sin.
No patience. When circumstances or other people get in the way of my best-effort agenda, I can't handle it. I get upset, lash out, become discouraged, or demand immediate change.	**Patience.** I have confidence that Christ is at work in me and others. I can trust his timing and his approval of me even when my efforts don't seem to be making much progress.

When the group is ready, share some of your results. Where do you sometimes sense your righteousness is found in yourself, even if you know better? How do you want to grow in confidence in Christ?

WRAP-UP AND PRAYER *10 MINUTES*

As part of your prayer time together, thank God for all that Christ freely gives you, and pray for confidence in him.

7

MATURITY

BIG IDEA

Because Jesus has already secured our way to glory, we press on to become more holy.

BIBLE CONVERSATION *20 MINUTES*

Paul has just finished using himself as an example of how no amount of good behavior or religious zeal can make us right with God. The righteousness that saves us is Christ's perfect righteousness, counted as ours when we have faith in him. We put our confidence in Jesus, not in our own achievements or effort.

However, this does not mean the Christian life is without effort. Rather, freed from the insecurity of having to earn our way, we work alongside God as he keeps using us and making us more holy. Again, Paul will use himself as an example, urging us to strive to live up to who we already are in Christ. He will call this a mature way to think, which oddly begins with admitting we are not yet as mature as we should be. Have someone read **Philippians 3:12–21** aloud, and then discuss the questions below:

First, notice the many things this passage says about underlying *belief*. What things does a mature Christian believe about himself and Christ, and why are they important?

Now, look at *attitudes*. What attitudes toward the Christian life will a mature believer have, and do any of these surprise or challenge you?

Verses 18–21 contrast the difference between the finish line for a citizen of heaven and the end point for an enemy of Christ. What do you find helpful about those finish line descriptions, and why?

****

Now take turns by paragraph reading the article aloud. When you finish, discuss the questions that follow.

Lesson

ARTICLE

PRESSING ON IN FAITH

5 MINUTES

When we read the Bible and come across a command, our flesh imme-diately wants either to condemn us for not obeying or to puff us up with pride because we think we are obeying pretty well. Because of this danger, we need a gospel lens through which we read God's com-mands. We need to see that Scripture tells us both *who we are* in Christ and *who we are becoming* in Christ.

For a believer, the *who we are* part is done. Jesus obeyed God's com-mands perfectly. He took the full weight of our sin, including our sinful desire to find our own righteousness, and he died for it—and gives us his perfect record. This amazing truth about who we already are frees us as we read about *who we are becoming*—the commands.

We know that even if we struggle to make progress in an area of obe-dience, God will complete the work he has started in us. What Jesus did for us was enough to secure our way to God. No matter where you are today, God is not surprised or worried. He has determined your destiny and secured it through the finished work of Christ. "For by a single offering, he has perfected for all time those who are being sanctified" (Hebrews 10:14). *Who we are* always comes before *who we are becoming.*

Paul talks about his sanctification process (becoming more holy) using images of a marathon. He says he is pressing on, straining toward what is ahead, trying to win a prize. He does not mean that he is unsure where he stands with God, but that he is aware he has a long way to go. Paul does not sleep spiritually. He takes seriously the areas of his life that do not align with Christ. He knows that Christ has secured his future glory, so he can keep pushing heavenward.

By gospel faith, this word is for us too. Because of what Christ has done for us, we can push forward with Paul. Neither our successes nor our failures in the race define us. In fact, Paul tells us to forget what lies behind. He does not mean that sin no longer matters, only that it cannot change our identity in Christ. We can own our sin, confess it, accept God's grace, and then forget it. We fix our eyes on Jesus, and we trust that what he has done for us is enough to guarantee that we will make progress as we keep moving forward.

Paul tells us that pressing on in our sanctification is what maturity in faith looks like. *Maturity* is not the same as perfection—it does not mean "without flaws." Paul is talking about us being full-grown Christians who know both our identity in Christ now and where Christ is taking us. Immature Christians either think they are already as good as they need to be, or they think they will not make it to the finish line because of their repeated failure.

But we know that what Christ has done for us is enough to get us all the way home, so seeing our imperfection is another chance to glory in him. Mature Christians do not need to fear being shown where they are falling short. Who we are in Christ is secure. We can be willing to listen to what our problems are.

As a young man, immature in my faith, I did not want to hear that I had problems. I thought I was nearly perfect. I mean, I had studied the Bible. I had a master's degree. I was a pastor. I was working very hard. At age twenty-seven, I was perfect. And then I grew up.

In those early years, my patient wife was reluctant to start an argument with me. She knew if she brought up some way that perhaps I was not as perfect as I envisioned myself, it would be very difficult for her to convince me. But a friend suggested I should ask some questions. He said, "Ask your wife: if there were one thing you could change about me, what would that be?" Well, at first, she didn't want to answer, because she knew I would argue. But eventually she said, "You're always angry." And of course I said, "No, how can you say that?"

But I did listen. And she was right. We need people to speak truth into our lives, and when Barbara spoke into my life, God used it powerfully. I hated it. It was embarrassing. It was hard. It was humbling. I did not change quickly. I had to admit that I had a long way to go. I had to put behind me all the things I thought were good. I had to believe that Christ had made me his own, and loved me anyway. And so I moved forward.

I am old enough now to see how God is changing me. I am no longer angry as I used to be. It means I treat people as I should. That did not make me a Christian; that came out of my life because I was a Christian.

This is the pattern of the Christian life. We move ahead. We take God's love. We ask for his forgiveness. We ask for his help, and he sends the Holy Spirit, and we move on. Some of the sins we struggle with are very hard, but we fight to not let those sins define us. We put them off and take hold again of Christ, who could not love us one iota more than he does right now even in our struggles.

We move forward into new patterns of living. We might even smile and be encouraged when our imperfection is revealed, because it means the gospel just gets bigger for us. Grace becomes even more astonishing. And our longing for heaven intensifies all the more, as it is our true home.

DISCUSSION *10 MINUTES*

The article mentions three marks of a mature Christian:

1. You admit you still have much to work on in striving against sin.

2. You have confidence in Christ that you will grow and reach the finish line.

3. You engage in the fight against sin, running hard.

Based on this, how has God given you maturity, and how would you like to become more mature?

Who is close to you and can help you see what sin you need to strive against? How well do you listen?

STRIVING IN PRAYER

20 MINUTES

For a mature Christian, striving to become more like Jesus begins with the neediness inherent in prayer. Verses 10–11 at the end of the last lesson's passage make a good framework for prayer. There, Paul says his goal for life in Christ is "that I may know him and the power of his resurrection, and may share his sufferings, becoming like him in his death, that by any means possible I may attain the resurrection from the dead."

On your own, follow the prompts below to create some prayer points for yourself based on Paul's outline of what it means to know Christ. Summarize some items you might pray for yourself as you run hard to be like Jesus. Make them items you're also willing to share with the group at the end of the exercise.

The power of his resurrection. By his victory over sin and death, Jesus has already given you a new life that defines who you are: the forgiveness and righteousness you enjoy, the love you have as a child of God, and God's power at work in you to say no to sin. This *who-you-are* power lets you run after holiness without fear, making it your own. So pick an aspect of how God has first made you his own, and pray that God would teach you about its full wonder.

Summary of my prayer to know how fully I belong to Christ: _____

_____

_____

_____

_____

Share in his sufferings. Your hard times, disappointments, and troubles do not go to waste but are used by God. He works within them to draw you closer to him, to teach you obedience, to confirm that Jesus is your brother, and to give you joy amid hardship as you follow Jesus's path in battling the temptations that come with human life in this world. So pray about trouble or suffering you face, that God would use it to train you to be like Jesus.

Summary of my prayer that God would use my sufferings: _____

_____

_____

_____

_____

Becoming like him in his death. Growth in holiness is about dying to yourself. You need to humble yourself so you listen to others and to God as they point out your sin, and then you need to kill off your own selfish interests as you love others and serve Christ. So pray about some way you want to listen better, admit your sin, put aside selfishness, or be willing to follow Jesus in a lose-your-life-for-his-sake manner.

Summary of my prayer about a way to die to myself: _____

_____

_____

_____

_____

That by any means possible I may attain the resurrection from the dead. In your race to be more like Jesus, you are encouraged not only by *who you are* but also by the promise of *who you are becoming* and the certainty that Jesus will raise his faithful ones to new life with him. That life is your prize, heaven is your upward call, and that hope can keep you a diligent follower of Jesus until the day you die or he returns. So pray about some way you want God to take your mind off earthly things and replace it with an eagerness for the glory to come.

Summary of my prayer for greater hope in the coming glory: _____

_____

_____

_____

_____

When the group is ready, tell about some of your prayer points. What will you be praying for as you strain toward the goal of becoming more like Jesus?

WRAP-UP AND PRAYER *10 MINUTES*

As the article pointed out, listening to people who are close to you and can point out your sin is a practice that shows maturity. So, consider who else you might share your prayer points with, or who you might ask what you need to add to the list. Begin the process of humbling admitting needs together by praying with your group for items on each other's lists.

8

UNITY

BIG IDEA

The gospel helps us face the threats of division among God's people.

BIBLE CONVERSATION *20 MINUTES*

In chapter 3, Paul explained the gospel. He wrote about how we are (1) given Christ's righteousness and (2) transformed into people who strive as citizens of heaven to be like Christ. Now in chapter 4, Paul will apply the gospel. He will mention several members of the Philippian church by name, urging them to help resolve an interpersonal conflict. Note that one of these is a person called Syzygus, which can be translated as "companion" or "yokefellow," so it might be his name or nickname or it might be a description of his role in Paul's ministry. Regardless, Paul enlists him to help resolve the conflict.

Have someone read **Philippians 4:1–9**, or have a few readers take turns. Then discuss the questions below.

What reasons does Paul give for why the Philippians should settle the conflict in the church? How does Paul's approach differ from ways you've seen other leaders respond to conflicts?

How would the instructions given in verses 4–9 be helpful for people who need to resolve a conflict?

Does Paul's instruction in verses 4–9 make you feel condemned, or eager to grow to become more like what he describes? Explain.

****

Next, read this lesson's article. Take turns by paragraph reading it aloud, and then discuss the questions that follow.

Lesson

ARTICLE

STANDING FIRM
5 MINUTES

When our kids were school-aged, Barbara and I spent some years living as missionaries in Ireland. We had been trained for cross-cultural living and made no assumptions that our Alabama accents would go unnoticed. As expected, there were a lot of laughs (mostly at ourselves) as the simplest of daily tasks suddenly were the most challenging undertakings we could imagine. But we were excited to be a part of how God was advancing his kingdom in that place, and to this day we feel incredibly honored to have been invited into our Irish friends' hearts and homes.

For our family, one of the most meaningful parts of making a home in another culture was how God mysteriously united us with missionary teammates who had done the same. But that does not mean everything within our team was fun or easy. Within a few months of our arrival, I got into a conflict with another missionary on the team. I was angry with him for some things he had said about what I should and should not be doing. I asked if we could talk, so we arranged to meet later that day in the park. As the time approached, I had a hard time imagining it would not come to blows.

As it turned out, we managed to smooth it over. But as time went on, it became obvious to everyone around us that we still were not getting along well. Eventually, we found ourselves at a retreat where one of our friends had to pull us aside. God used this friend to help us get to the root issues and find a way forward. That was nearly thirty years ago. This teammate and I have been working together most of the time since then, and we have become very good friends. God worked in that conflict to transform our relationship and make it constructive.

As we move into Philippians 4, Paul directly addresses the threat of division in the church. This is where the doctrinal rubber meets the road. Paul begs his friends in Philippi to stand firm in the Lord, calling up a picture of gospel unity based on the Roman army. Recall that Philippi was populated by retired Roman soldiers. A major factor in Roman military success was their strict formation. Huddled together closely in lines, they would only move forward together. No soldier dared break ranks, as it would compromise the strength of the formation. They literally conquered the world by standing together.

Paul wants us to see how vital gospel unity is in the church. We worship with people who are different from us. We are not united in the way we look, dress, or vote. But we have been united in Christ, and we have been given his mindset. This mindset says we can lay down our lives in order for others to experience the love of God. We can stand firm together in the Lord—on his promises, in his righteousness, as citizens of his kingdom. The gospel is sufficient for unity.

Paul would not have been surprised to know about the conflict with my teammate. It is well documented that the number one reason missionaries leave the field is conflict with other missionaries. Our churches, too, experience conflicts, division, and polarization. That was the case in Philippi, so Paul addresses it head-on. He pleads with each woman separately, by name, to consider all that is true about them because of Jesus and to be of the same mind "in the Lord."

In the Lord, we have the righteousness of Christ, which frees us from having to win an argument. It frees us to move toward one another in love and not demand that the other meet our needs, because Jesus has already met our greatest need. Paul praises the women because they have helped in his missionary work, reminding them that together they are partners in the gospel. Steeping ourselves in the gospel of Christ Jesus is the only antidote to division and polarization in the church.

So as Paul moves on, he steeps us in the gospel again. In verse 4, he calls us to rejoice in the Lord, and then says it again in case we missed it. While most of our Bibles start a new paragraph here, I think there is actually a direct connection to the unity Paul was just talking about. Rejoicing in the Lord is part of how the gospel gets into our hearts and helps us know how to move forward when relationships feel sticky.

Tim Keller has written about how rejoicing, in the Bible, means something much deeper than simply being happy about things: "'Rejoicing' is a way of praising God until the heart is sweetened and rested, and until it relaxes its grip on anything else it thinks that it needs."* Rejoicing in the Lord helps us come back to our senses and return to gospel sanity. And as we rejoice together in the Lord, that is when the Christian community begins to shine and look really different to people outside.

One time, two of our missionaries were in a Jeep in the jungle of Uganda, along with a local guide. The Jeep broke down, and soon the two missionaries got into a heated argument over how to handle the situation. They finally fixed the Jeep and began the journey home. After a period of silence, the missionaries began talking. They repented to each other and were reconciled. The guide, who was in the back seat, witnessed it all and told them, "I have never seen anything like that before." It is what drew him to Christ. As we stand firm in

---

* Timothy Keller, *Counterfeit Gods: The Empty Promises of Money, Sex, and Power, and the Only Hope that Matters* (New York: Penguin, 2009), 173.

the Lord, with the same mind in the Lord, rejoicing in the Lord, the light of the gospel shines in a dark place.

DISCUSSION *10 MINUTES*

When conflict with other believers arises, how often is your first response to remember who you are in the Lord? How might your conflicts end differently if you did that more often?

When have you seen conflict between believers handled well, so that it was a gospel witness to others?

Lesson

EXERCISE

"PRACTICE THESE THINGS"

20 MINUTES

Paul says, "Practice these things." His list of instructions in our passage is a helpful part of resolving conflict and having unity with each other. Rejoicing, praying, thinking about what is praiseworthy, and so on will not mean you avoid conflict altogether. But when these practices are your habits, they will help you settle conflicts when they arise. They are practices of confidence in Christ, which frees you from being a confidence-in-self person who needs to get your way.

On your own, read about each of Paul's instructions below. You'll then pick a few that you can practice with certain other believers. Be ready to discuss your responses at the end of the exercise.

PAUL'S LIST OF PRACTICES

Rejoice. Songs of praise crowd out complaining. Christians are a people who sing when they are worried and turn to praise when they are weary. You rejoice *always*, even in hard times, rejoicing *in the Lord* over his love for you that transcends all evils.

Be reasonable. Paul commends gentleness as a habit for living among everyone. You can be patient with others, asking questions, listening, not making every incident a this-means-everything cause for strife that you must win—because you know the Lord is at hand. He is near you today win or lose, and he is coming soon to set all things right.

Pray. Paul describes prayer as the alternative to anxiety. Prayer overcomes protect-yourself panic and brings the peace of God. You can trust God who "will supply every need of yours" (v. 19). Prayer guards your heart and your mind from feeling you have to make others fit your plans to fix your problems.

Be thankful. Gratitude is a heart attitude within prayer. You are thankful that your Father surely loves you, delights to hear from you, and will answer in a way that's good for you. Thankfulness relieves the pressure of things having to turn out the way you think is best.

Think about praiseworthy things. Paul says to interrupt bad thoughts with beautiful ones. Instead of letting the concerns and amusements and arguments of the world flood over you, you take control of what consumes and comforts you. You make it a practice to take in the purer and far more excellent gospel story.

Imitate godly people. Part of humility is a willingness to learn from others who know Christ. When you realize you are still a trainee under the care of your Good Shepherd and his undershepherds, your bluster recedes. You regularly place yourself under God's Word, and you find mentors and friends who do the same.

As we've seen from Paul, the practice of these things often happens *in community*, as you live and worship and even struggle with fellow believers. So now, consider *how* you will practice these things, and *with whom*. Pick items from the list above to fit the prompts below.

By myself, personally, I especially want to work on practicing these items from Paul's list:

1. _____

2. _____

With a friend or godly mentor (or perhaps a spouse/family), I'd like to be intentional about practicing these items from Paul's list:

1. _____

2. _____

In the larger assembly of God's people, I want to be committed to regularly practicing these items from Paul's list:

1. _____

2. _____

With a believer I've had some conflict with (which again may mean a spouse or family member), I want to make a point of practicing these items from Paul's list:

1. _____

2. _____

When the group is ready, share some of your responses. How will you practice Paul's list, and with whom? Explain your choices and why you picked them.

Each of these practices is not first of all about trying hard to change yourself, but about remembering and believing the goodness of Jesus. What might you do to keep that in mind as you practice these things?

WRAP-UP AND PRAYER *10 MINUTES*

Take time to engage in the practice of prayer right now with your group, remembering that it is the alternative to anxiety. What are you anxious about? (Maybe you're even anxious about the instruction you've just received through the Bible.) Pray about it together, with thanksgiving, knowing that your Father gives you all good things.

Lesson

9

CONTENTMENT

BIG IDEA

As we continue to live into our relationship with Christ, he becomes enough for us.

BIBLE CONVERSATION *20 MINUTES*

Throughout his letter to the Philippians, Paul has reminded us of all that the gospel means for us as believers—and all it can mean for the watching world. And now as Paul closes the letter, we get to see in Paul himself the cumulative effect of the gospel. He will start to thank the Philippians for the gift they sent him while he is in prison, brought by Epaphroditus. But the thought of this will cause him to switch gears and write about another topic: contentment. And so, we will see what happens in our lives when the gospel takes hold of us and we increasingly live by its promises.

Have someone read **Philippians 4:10–23**, or have a few readers take turns. Then discuss the questions below:

Based on this section of his letter, what are some ways Paul might finish the sentence, "I am most thankful for _____." How does it differ from what you might be thankful for if you received a much-needed gift?

When Paul says he can do all things through the Lord's strength, what challenges does he have in mind? Why are they difficult?

How do an eagerness to sacrifice (v. 18) and a confidence that God will supply (v. 19) work together in your life?

＊＊＊＊

Now take turns reading this study's final article aloud, switching readers at each paragraph break. Then discuss the questions that follow the article.

Lesson

ARTICLE

CHRIST ALONE
5 MINUTES

When Barbara and I first started planting churches, we lived in the small town of Jonesville, Louisiana. The church there was in a large farmhouse built on a floodplain, so the first floor was just concrete blocks and was quite bare, while the church met on the second floor. But when we moved there with our family, the church converted that concrete-block first floor into an apartment that became our home. There were two bedrooms for us and our three small children. It was pretty tight.

There was no separate door to the second floor where the church met, just stairs from our first-floor apartment. That got interesting on Saturday mornings when a men's prayer breakfast met upstairs. Men from the church would come, but they would also invite men from the community. Everyone in town was curious about who we were, why we would come there, and how the church could possibly have made that basement into an apartment. So there was Barbara with the little ones, trying to enjoy their Saturday morning sleep-in while I joined the men, having no idea the men in the church planned to come through and show our living situation to all those curious people in the community.

It was a bit of a "rude awakening," to be sure. Barbara knew there would be sacrifice involved for our family as we moved to that place and engaged in ministry. But at times, the way the situation had turned out gave us real pause.

As we know, the apostle Paul had his share of struggles too. But he says he has learned a secret: contentment, no matter his circumstances. As he writes, Paul is still in jail and yet content. Our Louisiana basement apartment situation was not jail, and yet we were not content. How can Paul be content?

Well, notice how when Paul starts to thank the Philippians for their gift, he begins by saying, "I rejoice in the Lord." He doesn't say, "I'm very glad that now I have some things I need." Their gift is not first of all about his needs. He's more excited about the Philippians' Christlike response. The big issue for him is seeing how his friends serve God, rejoicing in the Lord, and living in the mystery of being content with that. Paul had Christ.

When we feel discontentment, it means we want something more than just Christ. Our hearts are driven by all sorts of other things. But Paul says he has learned contentment, and our hearts can learn too. We can let our discontentment be our warning sign. If our joy dies and peace is gone, we know that our hearts are valuing something more than Christ in that moment. We have forgotten the gospel. We have forgotten God's love for us.

Paul learned contentment through life experience. When God brought plenty, Paul had to learn to be content in God himself and not get his satisfaction with life from the plenty he had. And when Paul had very little or was hungry, he had to learn to be content in God and not grumble and complain. He learned how to return to Jesus when things were going well, and he learned how to return to Jesus when things were going terribly. He learned how to repent and believe in Christ alone regardless of circumstances. He learned how to rejoice in the Lord and delight in the person and work of Jesus.

Being content is a matter of the heart. This is something God teaches us along the way in all the circumstances we face. Through different stages, both struggles and victories in life, we can learn the sacred secret of being content. As we repeatedly connect our hearts to Christ, we become free both from the love of money and from anxiety about money. We learn that he is the only one who can bring us peace, joy, and contentment.

Paul opens up to the Philippians because he wants them to have that same contentment—to have a heart at peace regardless of circumstances. He reveals the secret of contentment in verse 13: "I can do all things through him who strengthens me." I have often heard this verse used out of context, but the context Paul is speaking about is the struggle to learn contentment. It is very difficult to be content in Christ when we have plenty, because it is very easy to trust our possessions more than we trust Christ. Paul says Christ strengthened him so that he could be content in Christ even if he had a lot of money.

Our hearts tend to love things. It would be easy for my attention to be moved from Christ to things. But I can do all things in Christ, so that my heart is not seduced to love what I have. Instead of holding on to it for life, I can hold on to it with an open hand before God and trust him for what I have. Like Paul, we can do all things in Christ. We can even have things without loving them.

We might try to find contentment elsewhere, but there actually is nowhere else. We only gain contentment as we trust that Christ is enough. The outcome of all that Paul has been pushing the Philippians to lay hold of, all through this letter, is this mysterious contentment that even penetrates a jail cell. This is what I desire for you too as we complete this study: that you would find God to be large enough, so that whether you have a lot or a little, you don't live in worry or fear. God is with you and he will meet your needs.

DISCUSSION *10 MINUTES*

When has your discontent helped you see you were wanting something more than Christ?

Which seems to take your eyes off Christ more quickly: worry about having little, or the love of having much? Explain.

Lesson

9

EXERCISE

GOING-FORWARD QUESTIONS

20 MINUTES

The final section of Philippians not only wraps up some key themes but naturally makes you look forward. This exercise will give you three going-forward questions, based on Paul's final thoughts, for you to ponder as you move beyond your study of Philippians. In mature gospel living, the three questions go together. They are about being content in Christ, receiving from Christ, and sacrificing for Christ—and those habits hang on each other. But for now, you will pick just one of the questions to consider.

On your own, read through each question and description below. Pick <u>one</u> to focus on, and then take some time with God. These are questions to consider carefully and prayerfully. So spend several minutes quietly in prayer, asking God to show you how you might answer the question you picked. After a while, you'll share your thoughts with the group.

CONTENTMENT. What have you seen about Jesus during your study of Philippians that lets you be content in him alone?

Christ is your starting place. Jesus is good enough, and has given you enough, that you can be safe and satisfied whether your worldly comforts are many or few. How have you grown, or how do you hope to grow going forward, in your joy in the gospel?

SUPPLY. What do you want God to give you?

Your Father is rich and generous, and he is eager to supply everything you need. You can take any need to him, but think especially about the finest prizes that make up the heavenward call: nearness to God and a Christlike life. What do you want God to give you or work in you, that you will persistently ask him to do going forward?

SACRIFICE. What is God calling you to give up for him, others, or the cause of Christ's mission?

The wonder of God's call on your life is that as you die to yourself and give to others, God is glorified in you and receives praise. You become a partner with Christ in his mission and in his sufferings that lead to new life. Going forward, how might you take yourself low to love others and raise high the name of Jesus?

When the group is ready, tell which question you picked and some of what you are thinking. How did it feel to spend time with your Father, or what did he teach you as you prayed? What is your chief going-forward application from Philippians?

WRAP-UP AND PRAYER *10 MINUTES*

You might end by going back to Paul's opening prayer in 1:9–11. Along with Paul, pray for each other that, going forward, your love would abound more and more and you would be filled with the fruit of the righteousness you have in Christ, to the glory and praise of God.

LEADER'S NOTES

These notes provide thoughts and background information that relate to the study's discussion questions, especially the Bible conversation sections. The discussion leader should read these notes before the study begins. Sometimes, the leader may want to refer the group to a point found here.

However, it is important that you not treat these notes as a way to look up the "right answer." The most helpful and memorable answers usually will be those the group discovers on its own through reading and thinking about the Bible text. You will lose the value of taking time to look thoughtfully at the text if you are too quick to turn to these notes.

LESSON 1: IDENTITY

Both Lydia and the jailor demonstrate an immediate and deep connection to Paul and Silas once they are converted, and this flows from the connection they all have to Jesus. Lydia treats the visitors like family, inviting them to live with her specifically because of her new status as their sister in Christ: "If you have judged me to be faithful to the Lord, come to my house and stay" (Acts 16:15). The jailor also invites them into his home and feeds them at his table, like family, with Acts 16:34 emphasizing his joy over the new person he has become. Core identities are transformed when a person believes the gospel.

The labels Paul uses for himself and the Philippian believers may need some explanation. To be a "servant" (*doulos*) of Christ could also be translated as "slave" or "bondservant," all of which indicate a person who is subject to do work assigned by a master. It was a life-defining status within ancient Greco-Roman culture. Often, over time, a *doulos* could earn enough to purchase their freedom. In some cases, they would even choose to remain part of their master's household. It's important to recognize that this institution, which was still prone to sin and abuse, was very different from the race-based, chattel slavery that was practiced in Europe and the Americas later in history. To be a "saint" (*hagios*) simply means to be one of God's holy people, set apart for him. Paul, Timothy, and the Philippian believers are servants of Christ and saints in Christ. Their whole lives are defined by Christ. They enjoy grace from him. They have peace because of him. They are children of the Father through him. And they know the belongingness of his lordship over them.

LESSON 2: CONFIDENCE

This part of Paul's letter contains words like *all, always, more,* and *filled.* Paul's joy and his prayers are both constant and far-reaching. Thinking about and praying for his Philippian friends deeply encourages him, and perhaps he does it so often because it helps him cling to Jesus all the more in his own suffering. The reason he can think and pray in such big ways about them is that he knows the bigness of salvation. Paul rejoices over the gospel's work "from the first day until now" and forward "to completion at the day of Jesus Christ." Jesus's saving work is comprehensive. He has done everything necessary to tear down the otherwise impenetrable barrier of sin between each individual and God, and to unify his people. Our past justification, ongoing sanctification, and future glorification are all of, by, and through God (see Romans 8:29–30; Ephesians 2:8–10). Paul knows from his own experience that people do not seek God, they reject him (see Romans 3:10–11). But God, in his great love, brings salvation from promise to fullness, from beginning to end.

Like his faith, Paul's affection is grounded in God. His love for the Philippians expresses itself in thanks and petition to God. It holds its place in his heart because of his and the Philippians' common experience of God's grace and their common mission to tell about Jesus. He actually swears by God that his own affection is the very "affection of Christ Jesus" (v. 8). He's saying in essence, "Not only do I love the Philippians, but God loves them through me." For Paul, sharing in God's grace leads to this kind of connection. Paul has been near to Jesus and constantly mindful of the gospel—and Jesus has rubbed off on him.

It makes sense, then, that Paul prays for the Philippians' love to abound more and more. Love is the outward expression of gospel faith (see Romans 13:8–10; Galatians 5:6). Paul sees beyond this world and its circumstances, to the fullness of what Jesus does for us. Jesus makes us like himself, loving like he loves. What a goal: to grow in the knowledge of God and in discernment about how to love each other best; to be pure and filled with the fruit of righteousness; to bring glory and praise to God until the day Jesus returns, and beyond! That life is our *more* and our *all*.

LESSON 3: SUFFERING

Even faced with a pending life-or-death verdict, Paul has several desires that matter more to him than that outcome. He rejoices to see the gospel advance and Christ proclaimed, even if it isn't done by him or in his way. He also wants to see the Philippians grow in the gospel. And his desire for himself, personally, is to be with Christ but not be selfish about that. He sees himself as a servant of Christ, not just a recipient of an easier life. This means that his goal as he faces the prospect of death is "that I will not be at all ashamed" (1:20). Death can be frightening, even for Paul, and he does not want to lose his courage. He wants to stay strong, keeping his joy and his grip on Christ, never failing out of fear to make his testimony for Christ. *How* he dies—strong in Christ—matters more than *if* he dies.

The result of this surrender to Jesus is peace and joy. That's a point Paul will make throughout the epistle. No matter what the tribulation, the presence of Christ means we can rejoice.

Paul wants the Philippians to know this same joy (v. 25), and so he encourages them to remain "standing firm in one spirit" (v. 27). A self-first life divides, but a Christ-first life unites us in the gospel. This is part of the freedom of the heart that Christ gives. Working side-by-side for the faith is a great witness in the world, a way not to be frightened by our opponents, and a way to gain assurance that God really is giving us salvation. When we stand firm with courage and stand together in love, people take notice and we are encouraged.

LESSON 4: HUMILITY

The Christian community Paul describes both flows from the blessings we share in Christ and imitates Christ. And if we follow Paul's example in this passage, it also gets its strength to carry on by looking at Christ and all that he is. It is only through Christ, who is unlike anyone else in both his humiliation and exaltation, that we can form a community unlike any other.

This passage may raise questions about exactly how Christ is unique, especially in how he is both God and a man. The Bible teaches that Christ is the Son of God, the second person of the Trinity. This means he is fully God in every way: eternal, all-powerful, unchanging, etc. To accomplish our salvation, the Son of God also became fully human in every way: bodily needs, human emotions, the ability to suffer and die, etc.—but without sin. This did not at all diminish his being God. Rather, it means the one person Christ has two natures. He has both a divine nature and a human nature at the same time. These two natures come together in the one person, but they still maintain individual integrity so that Jesus is never less than fully God nor some kind of unreal superhuman. The two natures in Christ are necessary for him to be our Savior. Only a person with truly human weaknesses who rose above temptation could suffer the wrath of God in our place. And only a person with truly divine greatness could be the necessary sacrifice of infinite value (see Psalm 49:7–8) who was able to ride out God's wrath and continue being our Savior in every way.

It is in his role as the God-man who accomplishes salvation that the eternal Son of God humbled himself to be obedient unto death. During his time on earth, the person Jesus continued to be God and to act according to his divine nature in things like holding the world together, for example (see Colossians 1:15–17). But his divine nature was veiled to us most of that time. And in his human nature, he was born, suffered, died, was buried, rose, and was exalted—as Paul sings about so eloquently. In fact, only someone who is both God and man in a single person could humble himself so extremely and be exalted so marvelously.

LESSON 5: MISSION

Your group may want further evidence that "work out your own salvation with fear and trembling" does not mean works righteousness—having to be good enough to earn God's eternal forgiveness. Point out how verse 13 highlights the way even our sanctification (a part of salvation we cooperate in) is first of all a work of God that he undertakes for his own glory and pleasure. And Paul will make it extra clear in 3:3–11 that we should put no confidence in even the most impressive outward obedience. Rather, the way to be found in Christ is not by having a righteousness of our own, but by having a righteousness that comes from God and is by faith (3:9).

Yet, we have the honor of becoming Christlike and shining "as lights in the world." This is a high calling. When things are dark, light is particularly strong. When things are hard, this new way of living becomes much more obvious. And notice that Paul has the whole world in mind. God wants to use our lives and testimonies further out than just in our town. We must have a view that includes faraway places. The Philippians had that, sending Epaphroditus to support Paul's travel-the-world ministry. In the same way, we too can extend our light into the whole world.

Such ventures fit a people whose mind is the same as that of Jesus, whose own mission was worldwide salvation. The privilege of carrying his gospel to the nations is one of the great joys of life in this era. We should be eager to do it like Epaphroditus, who had the same tireless fight and eye for people's needs as Christ. We should strive to do it like Timothy, who had the same genuine concern for the welfare of others as Christ. We should even be ready to do it like Paul, who had the same willingness to make himself a sacrificial offering as did Christ.

LESSON 6: JOY

Although the Old Testament law was a good gift from God, no system built on trying to earn a right record with God by our obedience can ever save anyone. The Judaizers were stressing law-keeping, especially certain external requirements that were part of the ceremonial law meant to point ahead to Christ (see Acts 15:1; Galatians 4:9–11). But to rely on any law-keeping to meet God's demands is a burden that will surely curse us, according to Galatians 3:10–14, as it keeps us from relying on Christ who alone kept God's law. And to cling to the ceremonial law after Christ has fulfilled it is an empty faith in heritage, not a saving faith in Jesus. Paul condemns the Judaizers because they attacked the heart of the gospel: that when our confidence is in Christ alone, we have the salvation we could never obtain otherwise.

Even if we know this, our sinful nature causes us to feel we need to supply our own credentials to God. We might tell ourselves we've earned God's approval by our right affiliations, right behavior, right passion, right sincerity, or right ceremonies. But this only leads us to confidence in ourselves, which brings arrogance or, more often, insecurity. Confidence in Christ, on the other hand, leads to the kind of life described in verses 10–11. Christ's death-defeating work has real power in us, making us confident that we are forgiven, loved, and guided in holiness. Freed from the pressure to save ourselves, we are able to die to ourselves, sacrifice for others, and endure until our Savior calls us home.

So, we receive Christ and his righteousness by faith. Be careful not to make faith itself into just another work. It's easy to start thinking our salvation depends on the strength of our faith, but that would be another way of trusting the flesh instead of trusting Christ. Faith is not about mustering up enough belief and trust, but about a posture of receiving from God. When our faith is in Christ, he is strong enough to save us even though our faith at times feels weak. Emphasize *whom* we trust, not how well we trust. Faith is inherently a posture for weak people.

LESSON 7: MATURITY

Paul moves from writing about *justification* in the first half of chapter 3 to *sanctification* in the second half. Both are aspects of the salvation we have in Christ, but there are differences. Justification is the legal act of God by which he forgives our sin and declares us righteous through faith based on Christ's work. We do not work for it; we *passively* rest from our works and receive it through faith in Christ. Sanctification is God's re-creative work in us to change our thoughts and desires so that our behavior becomes more righteous like Christ. God remains the author of our sanctification, but we become *active* in this part of salvation and cooperate with his work in us. It is a mistake to think either that God becomes distant and sanctification is all up to us (not so, see 1:6; 2:13), or that we can just relax and let God work (also wrong, as this passage makes clear). Rather, we work at our sanctification in a trusting-God way: knowing he is forever on our side, depending on the Holy Spirit's work in us, and sure that although sanctification remains incomplete in this life God will perfect us in the next.

Mature Christians believe these things, and this guides our attitude about the Christian life. We are both secure in our status in Christ and eager to live up to it, knowing that more lies ahead. We readily admit we need to grow in holiness and are excited about the process. We humbly imitate those who are further along. We are neither dispirited by failure nor lackadaisical after making some progress, but forget the past and strain forward. We think of heaven as our true home, and heavenly behavior as our true calling, so that fighting sin becomes an act of aligning with our true selves.

In all of this, gospel truths keep us focused. Not only do we have the comfort of eternal forgiveness in Christ, but also the hope of eternal life with Christ. Chapter 3 takes us from the starting line of the Christian life, where we receive our justification, to the finish line where we receive our glorified bodies. All of this makes us run eagerly after holiness—both to live out who God has already declared us to be, and to start living now like we will be in heaven.

LESSON 8: UNITY

Paul's reasons for wanting conflict in the Philippian church to be resolved go beyond general peacefulness or practicality. Conflict does not fit the gospel. The women who are at odds are fellow workers with Paul, people saved in Christ, and sisters he loves in the Lord. Therefore, he does not shame them for their dispute but speaks to them respectfully and caringly. He expects them to be able to work things out due to the spiritual life they have—not by worldly means, but "in the Lord." At the same time, he does not ignore their conflict, pretend everything is okay, or try to keep it hidden. In this way, Paul is like Jesus, who taught that if we realize our brother has something against us, we should leave mid-worship and go be reconciled immediately (see Matthew 5:23–24). Paul points to the women's membership in the church and enlists others to help resolve the problem. He approaches it seriously, lovingly, and cooperatively.

At the same time, Paul's solution is constantly *spiritual*. Conflict often flows from anxiety or from a feeling that we need things to go our way, which in turn comes from being self-reliant instead of Christ-reliant. So Paul urges the Philippian church to rejoice in Christ, know that he is near, give thanks, pray instead of letting anxiety linger, and think on the gospel—and so be guarded by the peace of God, which is the foundation for peace among ourselves.

All of this comes under the maturity mentioned in the previous chapter. Remember that part of Christian maturity means realizing we are not yet mature. With our condemnation removed in Christ, we can dare to look at Paul's description of the Christian life with eagerness about who we are becoming rather than despair over our failings.

LESSON 9: CONTENTMENT

Although Paul is glad to receive the Philippians' gift, the spiritual realities behind the gift matter more to him than the money itself. He rejoices in their concern (v. 10), their kindness (v. 14), their partnership with him in mission (v. 15), the fact that he sees fruit in their lives (v. 17), and the way they have pleased God by their sacrifice (v. 18). And for his part, he is more focused on the amount of contentment he has in Christ than the amount of money that arrived with Epaphroditus.

Not that this is easy for Paul. In fact, it takes the work of God in him for him to be content in Christ whether he has much money or none. When Paul says he can do all things through the Lord's strength, he means overcoming the anxiety and idolatry that arise over daily needs. To be content with our eternal blessings in Christ even when we are hungry is hard, but it happens when the Lord gives us strength. And to find our life and joy in Christ even when we have lots of earthly things is also hard (maybe harder!), but it too happens when the Lord gives us strength.

In the Bible, generosity is often connected to not being anxious about our own needs because we know God will care for us. Here, Paul commends the Philippians' sacrificial gift and then reminds them that God will supply what they need. They can give without worrying about their own needs because they know God provides. Jesus makes a similar point about anxiety over worldly needs in Matthew 6:24–34. On the flip side, a love of money means we are not trusting that God is with us and gives what we need: "Keep your life free from love of money, and be content with what you have, for he has said, 'I will never leave you nor forsake you'" (Hebrews 13:5). For more from Paul on money and contentment, see 1 Timothy 6:6–10.

mission
propelled by God's Grace

Since 1983, Serge has been helping individuals and churches engage in global mission. From short-term trips to long-term missions, we want to see the power of God's grace transform your own life and motivate and sustain you to move into the lives of others—particularly those who do not yet know Jesus. As a cross-denominational, Reformed, sending agency with more than 300 missionaries in 26 countries across 5 continents, we are always looking for people who are ready to take the next step in sharing Christ. Explore the life-changing opportunities for you to grow and serve around the world through:

- **Short-term Teams:** One- to two-week trips oriented around serving overseas ministries while equipping the local church for mission

- **Internships:** Eight-week to nine-month opportunities to learn about missions through serving with our overseas ministry teams

- **Apprenticeships:** Intensive 12–24 month training and ministry opportunities for those discerning their call to cross-cultural ministry

- **Career:** One- to five-year appointments designed to nurture you for a lifetime of ministry

 Grace at the Fray

**Visit us online at:
serge.org/mission**

resources for Every Stage of Growth

No matter where you are on your Christian journey, Serge resources help you live out the gospel in every part of your life and encourage the same growth in others.

Books and Studies

- **Personal and Small Group Study:** The Gospel-Centered Life and Gospel Transformation series (*Gospel Identity*, *Gospel Growth*, and *Gospel Love*) target real-life transformation grounded in robust, grace-based theology. Go deeper with our gospel-centered studies on community, work, parenting, and more. And, cultivate a gospel-centered lens on all of scripture with our book-specific Gospel-Centered Life in the Bible series.

- **Stories from the Field:** Books such as *Promises in the Dark*, *The Mission-Centered Life*, and The Rwendigo Tales series, written by Serge missionaries, will captivate your imagination and heart as they show how God advances His Kingdom in big and small ways through weak vessels who are changed by His grace.

- **Teens and Kids:** Whether you are a parent, youth worker, or a children's ministry teacher or volunteer, transformative resources such as *Show Them Jesus*, *The Gospel-Centered Life for Teens*, and the *What's Up?* curricula for middle and elementary students can help kids discover the gospel and build a relationship with the God who cares for them.

- **Ministry Leaders:** Pastors, missionaries, and others engaged in ministry can be so focused on the work that we forget our ongoing need for the same gospel message we preach to others. Books like *The Heart of a Servant Leader* and *Running on Empty* reorient our hearts and minds to the joy of belonging to Christ, even while providing practical guidance for ministry.

Discipleship and Training

- **Mentored Sonship:** Mentored Sonship is a one-on-one mentoring program that transforms what your head knows into what your heart needs—the life-changing message of the gospel. Over 16 lessons, a personal mentor will help you apply what you are learning to the daily struggles and situations you face, as well as model what a gospel-centered faith looks and feels like.

- **Discipleship Lab:** Disciples who are motivated and empowered by grace to reach out to a broken world are handmade, not mass-produced. Discipleship Lab is a 6-month, live discipleship training program that helps you gain the core theological understanding and practical discipling skills to help others experience gospel transformation in their lives.

 Grace at the Fray

Visit us online at:
serge.org/renewal

newgrowthpress.com

resources
for Continued Spiritual Growth

Every day around the world, Serge teams help people develop and deepen a living, breathing, growing relationship with Jesus. We help people connect with God in ways that are genuinely grace-motivated and increase desire and ability to reach out to others. Whether you are a church leader, actively engaged in ministry, or just seeking to go deeper in your relationship with God – we have resources that can help.

Grace-Centered Teaching Events

Both scripture and our own experience tell us that this side of heaven we will never outgrow our need for God's renewing grace. Serge was founded on the principle that missionaries and ministers of the gospel - whether vocational or not - need to hear and experience ongoing reminders of the gospel just as much as the ones they are trying to reach. Serge hosts periodic conferences as one way we seek to nurture this continual dynamic of grace leading to mission, including in North America. While the content and format of the weekends can vary, these events consistently feature transformative biblical teaching, authentic stories of how the gospel changes us, and small group interaction – all aimed at cultivating personal gospel renewal that frees you and propels you into missional living.

Webinars and Podcasts

Serge's webinars and podcasts are free and easy ways to regularly hear grace-centered teaching from a variety of presenters - both Serge and non-Serge. With a broad range of topics like parenting, personal growth, leadership, and ministry, these conversations will help you apply the gospel to more and more areas of your everyday life and relationships.

Books and Studies

Serge has a growing collection of grace-centered publications that bring together grace-based theology with materials and teaching to help you live out the gospel in every part of your life. Whether you are looking for personal devotionals, small group studies, guidance for ministry, or honest and compelling stories from the mission field, our books and studies can encourage your faith and help you grow in your understanding and experience of God's grace.

Serge Grace at the Fray

newgrowthpress.com

**Visit us online at:
serge.org/books-and-studies**